A
VISION
AND
A LEGACY

The Story of Mennonite Camping, 1920-80

by
Jess Kauffman

FAITH AND LIFE PRESS
Newton, Kansas

Library of Congress Number 84-8008611
International Standard Book Number 0-87303-094-X
Printed in the United States of America

Illustrated by Mary Erickson
Design by John Hiebert
Printing by Mennonite Press, Inc.

Publication has been made possible in part by a grant from the Schowalter Foundation.

To staff and campers who taught me so much about living, and who helped me believe in Christian camping;

And to my faithful wife, Vi, who supported me all the way; and to our children, Ivan, Leila, Wilma, Patricia, who shared unselfishly,

this story is dedicated.

FOREWORD

This study of the history of the camping movement in the Mennonite and Brethren in Christ groups is timely since the movement is now eighty years old. The first references to camping in the Mennonite church were in connection with the General Conference Mennonite mission to the Hopi Indians as early as 1903. The author, Jess Kauffman, is well qualified to write on this topic, for he is one of the pioneers who helped to nurture the growth of the movement into what it is today.

Mennonites and Brethren in Christ were quick to recognize the impact that retreats and camps were making on youth and children. The early programs emphasized evangelism and spiritual growth in the Christian faith. It is interesting to note that the outdoors, the natural environment, was not a primary focus of study, but rather was looked upon as a place or a setting where youth could be taught biblical truths and be encouraged to make a commitment to the Christian faith. Not until recently has emphasis been placed on using the outdoors, God's creation, as a primary resource to gain a better understanding of the nature of God. The latent potential of the natural environment as a teaching tool to promote spiritual growth is yet to be discovered. Many church-related camps of today are not capitalizing on one of their greatest assets, their setting, the outdoors.

Each summer, camping programs provide hundreds of young people the opportunity to gain experience in working with small groups as teachers and cabin leaders. Here in the informal atmosphere of the camp, young people can test their convictions and values and work on the development of leadership skills.

The varied programs of the camps and retreats across the churches have made their impact on many lives, both of campers and staff persons. Many are quick to point to experiences at camp as being significant in making some of the most important decisions of their lives. Thus, camping facilities and programs have grown to where we now have a camp or retreat program wherever clusters of Mennonites and Brethren in Christ are to be found across North America. Jess Kauffman indicates that a camp program exists for every 2,550 church members.

Mennonites and Brethren in Christ have always been interested in mission and service programs. Camping has provided them with an effective way to work with culturally deprived, mentally and physically handicapped, and delinquent children, as well as with people of our own groups.

It is interesting to note that a program with the potential of reaching children and youth in Christian growth and commitment, leadership development, and service opportunities has had such acceptance that there are now approximately a hundred different camping programs and facilities throughout the United States and Canada in the several conferences. Paradoxically, the church has not recognized the contribution of camping programs on the same level as other Christian education programs such as the Sunday school, vacation Bible school, and youth programs. While some of the districts have given strong support in both money and personnel to the camping program, none of the major Mennonite denominations have given camping a major role in allocation of funds or personnel. The Mennonite Camping Association, which is primarily supported by the Mennonite Brethren, Mennonite Church, and the General Conference Mennonite Church, is dependent entirely on contributions of volunteer staff and officers.

The Mennonite camping programs will continue to grow and to help develop leaders. Mennonite camping leaders have served as the president of the American Camping Association, as president of the National Council on Outdoor Education, as trustees for the Fund for the Advancement of Camping, and in leadership roles with Christian Camping International. They have made significant contributions to the National Council of Churches in their outdoor ministries programs.

This book, telling of the evolution of the camping movement among the Mennonites and Brethren in Christ, showing the hills and valleys in each of the decades, will have both historical and inspirational value to its readers.

Oswald Goering

PREFACE

During the summer of 1982 I was camping with my family along the Chena River north of Fairbanks, Alaska. To the north, and above timberline in the tundra we could see the Granite Tors. They were a challenge. The round trip would require a twenty-mile hike and a long day. I was aware that this could be my last climb up a mountain because I was in my seventies. But I wanted to climb one more mountain with the children. We had done it numerous times over the years. On this hike there would be grandchildren also. This would make it special.

My hiking technique was to pace myself so that it was not necessary to stop often to rest. But on this trip I would often stop for the express purpose of looking back at the panoramic view before me. It was spectacular. The higher the climb, the greater the view. When we reached the summit we could see peaks and valleys in other directions. I sat down to rest, to look, to worship. A voice seemed to say, "Old man, what are you doing up here on this mountain?" I replied, "Life is so much like this. Peaks and valleys. The two of them create a beautiful scene."

I see the movement of Christian camping and retreats in our Mennonite and Brethren in Christ churches as one of peaks and valleys. The panoramic view is beautiful. The peaks are outstanding and majestic. But the valleys are where the action is. That is where the miracles took place and where there was healing and restoration of soul and body. It was there that thousands of campfires lit up the evening skies, and where thousands of campers responded to the warmth of God's love.

In order to tell the story of Christian camping in the Mennonite and Brethren in Christ conferences of North America it was necessary to research a total of 136 camps, retreat centers, and programs that were using leased or improvised facilities, and that had beginnings as early as the 1920s. Included in the research and story are the Mennonite Church, the General Conference Mennonite Church, the Mennonite Brethren, the Brethren in Christ, and the Evangelical Mennonite Brethren.

The conferences have a combined membership of 229,320 in North America and operate a total of approximately ninety camps, retreat centers, and established programs using leased facilities. Thus there is one campground or program for each 2,550 members. This is a significant undertaking for relatively small denominations. The founders of yesterday did not plan it this way, but the outdoor ministry of Christian camping was an idea whose time had come, and God has used it in a remarkable way in the program of nurture and evangelism. Its contribution cannot be shown by graphs and charts, and other statistical information. It is evident in the story of its growth and acceptance and in the lives of many people.

Choice parcels of real estate totaling 8,836 acres are now owned by Mennonite camps. Some are on the shores of beautiful lakes, in the high mountains, or in the rolling hills of the countryside; some are found in peaceful settings on the plains or wherever the founders of camping were led in their search for a suitable location. God's leading in this choosing of locations would be a volume of miracles if the stories were all told. It was not unusual for the search to require years. In other instances the location was almost instant. This real estate was acquired when prices were only a fraction of 1980 values. Some of this land would not be available now at any price. Many of these properties border national forests or other public domain that can be utilized in the program. Several facilities have been developed in choice locations secured by long-term lease from government agencies, and on land that is not for sale or private ownership.

If all these facilities were filled to capacity at one given time there would be a total of 12,977 people benefiting from their programs. Many of these facilities are open the year-round, with many thousands of people coming and going. Others operate only in summer, and on other special occasions. Camps vary in size, from quite small to large. But size is not important; each camp is serving in the niche where God has planted it.

Operational overhead of the combined community of camps and retreats is in excess of fifteen million dollars a year. The major part of this amount is covered by camper and rental fees, although it is not uncommon for programs to be subsidized so that specialized programming for disadvantaged and handicapped children can be a part of this ministry. In other instances programs are subsidized by conferences as an outreach to children of the community.

The combined market value of this community of camps and retreats is approximately fifty-nine million dollars. Voluntary contributions of time and materials made development possible, but accounting did not usually reflect this. The total book values as shown on financial statements is thirty million dollars. This figure represents the total cash outlay, rather than the actual worth.

The story of the camping movement is not the story of an easy road. There were trails to blaze. Those who blaze trails often travel alone. It can be lonesome and frightening, with a future that is uncertain and unknown. It required men and women of faith and courage who forged ahead in spite of the obstacles. But God's timing was good. The church would be needing this outdoor ministry in the days ahead. We have blazed trails. We have labored in the valleys and reached summits. Ahead there are more peaks to climb, more valleys to cross. I welcome the opportunity of telling the story of the movement as it has unfolded in the Mennonite conferences of North America.

Jess Kauffman

TABLE OF CONTENTS

CHAPTER ONE

Setting the Stage

Events and Movements, 1890-1920
Which Affected Mennonite Life and Thought

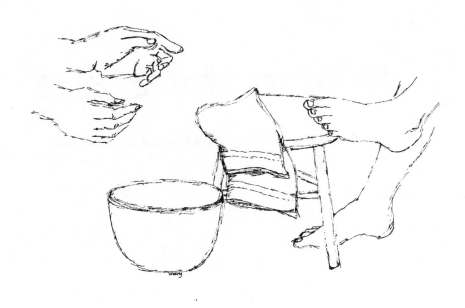

*The Mennonite emphasis on
servanthood, brotherhood, and peace,
along with conconformity to the world
influenced their life style, their philosophy,
and their strict adherence to what
they understood scripture to mean regarding
the "pleasures of the world."*

Setting the Stage

Holding camps and retreats within the Mennonite and Brethren in Christ churches of North America was not an isolated movement with a defined beginning all its own. It was closely related to and influenced by other events and movements both within the church and in society at large.

By 1900 organized camping had become an established institution in North America. Many church groups had adopted the program as part of their ministry to children and youth. Private camps were sponsored by those in the educational field. Agencies were providing outdoor living experiences for children. Campers were recruited from urban areas where families had been locating as the industrial revolution changed lifestyles, and families were moving from the farms into the cities.

The period of greatest expansion for organized camping was the three decades between 1910 and 1940. An early historian in writing of this movement during that time stated that the increase was attributed to the ever-growing revolt against the tyranny of modern city life, and to the effectiveness with which organized camping met children's needs for worthwhile outdoor activity.[1]

As early as 1872 welfare organizations had begun operating "fresh-air homes" in the country. Around the turn of the century many of these changed to fresh-air camps, and later evolved into camps stressing mental and physical growth as well as improvement of health and physical well-being. When this outdoor ministry was introduced into the Mennonite church it was a tested and tried institution that had been established as a North American tradition. It was waiting for its release into the program of nurture and evangelism within the church.

Influences Within the Church

During the period prior to World War I Mennonites and Brethren in Christ were still a basically rural people. As ethnic groups their needs were not the same as those of their urban neighbors. An outdoor ministry such as Christian camping was not in their thinking because it did not seem needed. As late as the 1950s parents of farm children would argue that camping was not necessary for their children because they got all the exercise they needed on the farm.

But these same people had a sense of community that was both beautiful and unique. They did not separate their lives into the secular and sacred. With their sense of servanthood, brotherhood, and mutual sharing they enjoyed fellowship and social interaction as they worked and worshiped. They got together to harvest crops, to build barns, or to plow the field of a sick neighbor. A neighbor would crank up a freezer of ice cream and invite everyone to come on over and enjoy the evening. They got together for cornhusking bees and quilting parties and made a party out of their work. They sang and played folk games. The young and the old enjoyed these times together.

It was during World War I that this way of life began to change. Many of the youth were uprooted and placed into circumstances for which they had not been prepared. Many experienced persecution. Some spent time in prison. Following the war in 1918 the Mennonite churches established an overseas relief program and sent young men to administer it. Among these was a young man by the name of Orie Miller, who later became a leading figure in the church and its activities. When he and others returned from this experience they had a changed sense of values, and began promoting activities for youth, especially the organizing of youth conferences. Though not in an official way, they influenced decisions which were made and provided leadership that brought about new thinking in the churches.[2]

This was also a time of migration from Russia and other parts of Europe for many Mennonite families who were establishing new homes in America. Others who had settled in the eastern part of the United States were pushing west and north. They traveled by train and wagon, on foot, or by boat. They homesteaded on the untamed plains of the West and built their homes of whatever materials were available, including the sod. The out-of-doors was a part of their lives. They found fellowship and recreation within that context.

It was a period of great awakening and growth for the churches. J. C. Wenger, Mennonite historian and churchman, says, "The great awakening was that spiritual revival which reached its high point in the American Mennonite Church between 1880-1910, which resulted in the adoption of new methods of work and in the launching of many new enterprises by the church . . . the great awakening was . . . the cause of many new methods of church work, including Sunday schools, evangelism, missions, and publications."[3]

During this time the Brethren in Christ youth movement emerged in 1907. The Mennonite Brethren who were still in Russia were active in their youth ministry. Within the Mennonite Brethren Church in America the *Jugendverein* was in existence and active. In the General Conference Mennonite Church the Christian Endeavor was "beginning to see the fruits." The Mennonite Church had its youth program, mainly the Young

People's Bible Meeting, a Sunday evening event. Sunday schools for all ages were common in all congregations.[4]

How the Camping Movement Began

The movement did not start at one place or with one group of persons. Like freckles on a face, camps and retreats just popped up everywhere. Each beginning had its own reasons and objectives. As the movement spread and gained in popularity many groups had already organized programs and were using leased or improvised facilities. Programs usually preceded the establishment of permanent facilities. These facilities and programs were equally distributed across the map where there were Mennonite fellowships. By 1960 there was no area with a concentration of Mennonites that did not have access to a camping or retreat program and the development of permanent sites was on the increase.

In the beginning, camps and retreat centers started in very simple ways. The men and women involved in these early adventures had not thought of starting a movement. For instance, Allen Good, pastor of the Portland, Oregon, Mennonite Mission, started by taking boys and girls from the city into the country for a couple of weeks each summer. Another young pastor, Austin Keiser, in Ohio, had a concern for the young people in the church, and organized a retreat on the Bluffton College campus. Tillie Yoder Nauraine was teaching in a Christian day school among black children, and provided a summer camping experience for them on her parents' farm in Ohio. Elsewhere concerned church leaders were providing opportunities for youth to get together for fellowship and Bible study.

The retreats of the General Conference Mennonite Church and the institutes of the Mennonite Church were similar in nature. The Mennonite Brethren's *Jugendvereine* (youth fellowships) provided this experience for them. The retreat and institute movement was responsible for the beginning of some of the camps and retreat centers. At first the facilities of a campus or congregation were used. Where such programs had been accepted, retreat centers were developed as a place for them to meet. This was true of the Laurelville Mennonite Church Center in Pennsylvania where the popular twelve-day institute at Arbutus Park over a period of years was one of the factors leading to the establishment of the Center. This process was especially prevalent in the General Conference Mennonite Church where a strong retreat program preceded the development of church-owned facilities.

The mission program in the Mennonite conferences was the stimulation for the development of other camp facilities and programs.

This trend was evident in the camping ministry of the Mennonite Brethren whose zeal for outreach prompted them to establish camps in areas where they were involved in church planting. Mission pastors and workers were quick to see the outdoor ministry of camping as an effective tool for nurture and evangelism in connection with their ministry to city children. This led to the development of many of the permanent sites.

Sunday Schools and the Camping Movement

The story of the outdoor camping movement would not be complete without the background of the Sunday school movement and its relationship to camping. As early as 1912 the International Sunday School Association was responsible for the first permanent church camp at Lake Geneva in Wisconsin. The Sunday school had established itself in the churches as a permanent institution. Now it was to become a parent in helping bring another movement into existence that would strengthen its program through an outdoor ministry. These two institutions were destined to supplement each other and to reach the lives of youth for Christ and the church.

After the Sunday school had been accepted among the Mennonites and Brethren in Christ there was a need for conventions and conferences to promote the movement and to train and recruit workers. These became very popular and were supported by a segment of the church that was interested in Christian education and outreach. There was a freedom in these gatherings to promote new ways of Christian service. The seeds which were sown in these meetings resulted in the establishment of many of the camps and retreat centers now in the church. The Sunday school movement had opened the way for the laity to be involved in the teaching ministry and other leadership roles. It presented the first opportunity for the women of the church to become involved. It set the stage for another movement to emerge.

The role of the Sunday school has been praised by historians as being the major influence in the growth of the church. Historian J. A. Toews of the Mennonite Brethren says, "The significance of the Sunday school for the growth, and even survival, of the Mennonite Brethren Church can hardly be overestimated. Eighty percent of the church members come from the ranks of the Sunday School." S. F. Pannabecker, in writing a history of the General Conference Mennonite Church, says, "The importance of the Sunday School in the developing churches has been one of the most effective agencies in inaugurating congregations and in promoting conference relationships."[5]

The first camps, like the first Sunday schools, were promoted by individuals who were concerned with the "terrible plight" of boys. Frederick Gunn, credited with establishing the first camp, was headmaster of a private school for boys in Connecticut, and saw an opportunity to strengthen his program in this way. Other of the early pioneers in camping were disturbed by the way that well-to-do families let their boys run the streets in the summer while they vacationed in the hotels of the cities. They established camping programs in the interest of the boys' welfare.

The camping ministry has been the bridge which helped many youth cross from their Sunday school experiences into meaningful relationships with the church. While sharing about their experience in camping with boys and girls in the early 1920s, members of the Portland, Oregon, congregation told me that a number of their members had joined as the result of their camping experiences. Prior to beginning their camping program they had observed that the Sunday school was not challenging children as they grew older, and before they were integrated into the fellowship of the church they were gone. The camping program had bridged this gap for some of them. The Sunday school and the camping program were supplementing each other. This has been verified many times.

The following was written by a camper from Camp Friedenswald a number of years ago. It speaks for many.

> In about the fifth grade I went to camp for the first time. I was kind of homesick, but I cried when I left. I didn't know why I cried. But there was something special there I had never felt before. For this reason I kept coming back year after year. I looked forward to the summer season when I could again be united with that special feeling. Soon I learned what that feeling was—it was the presence of God in a Christian atmosphere. On this I built my faith.[6]

The Sunday school continues to make its contribution in teaching what the Word of God has to say about how the Christian life should operate. The outdoor ministry of Christian camping provides a laboratory in Christian living where these truths and principles can be put into practice. In Sunday school children and youth are taught to love their enemies, to accept all people, and to be thoughtful of others. The influence of the Christian camp and mature leadership aids the camper in growth and understanding of these principles of Christian living.

A camper once asked me, "What makes the atmosphere of camp so relaxing and meaningful?" We talked about it for a while, then concluded that it was one of those things experienced, but not easily put into words. Fortunate is the child who can experience the Sunday school and a Christian camp in those impressionable years.

CHAPTER TWO

The Twenties

A Decade of Beginnings

Like the grain of mustard seed,
the beginnings were small,
but grew into a tradition of nurture
and evangelism that spread to churches
across North America.

The 1920s in general was a decade of change in the social and economic lives of all Americans. The World War I armistice had been signed just prior to the decade. Society was riding on a wave of economic prosperity. Optimism was blind. It was a decade when new and radical social liberties were being accepted, establishing trends which have continued. Then suddenly this optimism and prosperity changed when the stock market crashed in October of 1929. Fortunes were lost. Mortgages were foreclosed. Savings were wiped out. Bread lines formed. So ended the golden twenties.

These national events are part of the story of the church and would affect its future. The life and thought of the youth were being influenced and shaped. They were asking questions about the church and about themselves. They were asking to be recognized as a part of the church. They were also looking beyond the church for some of their answers, and to many of them the grass looked greener on the other side of the fence. Church leaders were showing concern and asking, "How can the church retain the interest of its youth?"

It was during this decade that dialogue between the youth of the church and its leaders began. Activities and programs were initiated for youth, and youth began to assume leadership roles in these activities. Prior to this the youth programs were planned for the youth, but not by them. Caution was the key word.

A unique pattern in the General Conference Mennonite Church was the aggressive leadership of its youth. They were active on the floor during conference sessions and organized activities within the framework of the church. When it came time to purchase property and develop retreat grounds some of them had sufficient organization and strength to do it. Early in the decade, Austin Keiser, a young pastor in his early twenties, was advocating a program that would more actively draw young people into the circle of church life. In one of his presentations about the retreat movement he made this statement, "The rising church wants something to do. A new day is at hand, and the youth are the ones who can make it or mar it . . . the method of presenting this challenge only remains to be found, and in the young people's retreats is to be found the answer."[1]

Leadership by the youth in the Mennonite Church came about in a more cautious fashion, and later. The Young People's Problems Committee was instructed to study all existing young people's movements of the church, such as Christian Life conferences, events sponsored by the colleges on their campuses, the Literary Society movement, and the Young People's institutes. One of the active programs in some sections of the

MENNONITE CAMPING PROGRAMS BEGUN IN THE 1920s

This map shows the approximate locations of the 10
camping and retreat programs begun in the 1920s.
Beginning dates and names are shown in the
chronological listing for the 1920s.

■ Permanent facilities
O Improvised or leased facilities

church at that time was the literary society. It appears that this originated on the college campus and was introduced into communities by returning students. The programs of the literary societies were not necessarily religious, although they could be. They were organized by the young people themselves and combined social and academic activities. Debates, essays, readings, songs, and the like were typical. Programs used local talent. They provided a community activity that filled a need in its day. During this time there remained strong family ties. Most activities were planned for the entire church family who met and shared in these events. Sunday school picnics and church outings, as well as other special events, usually included the entire family. Summer Bible schools and clubs for boys and girls began to appear.[2]

The Mennonite Brethren were in a different phase of growth during this time. This was a time of migration for many, and a time of church planting in America. They were leaving their homes in Russia. Their youth programs were strong, and loyalty among their youth for the church was outstanding. Historian J. A. Toews comments, "One of the greatest spiritual assets of the Mennonite Brethren Church through the years has been a large, active youth group. Young people have often provided the vision and dynamic for blazing new trails in evangelism and Christian service."[3] During the first two decades of the twentieth century fellowship groups became generally accepted in the Mennonite Brethren churches of Russia. After the revivals in 1924-25, large youth festivals were also organized, though all such activities were terminated in the early years of the Stalin regime. This pattern was adopted by the churches as they came to America.

If a specific decade were chosen as the beginning of the outdoor ministry of Christian camping and retreats in the Mennonite conferences, it would be the 1920s. Like the grain of mustard seed, these beginnings were small, but grew into a tradition and ministry that has been felt throughout the churches.

Significant Beginnings in the 1920s

1920 - **Youth camping for Hopi Indians** in northern Arizona by *General Conference Mennonites* and others began this approximate date.

1922 - **Boys and Girls taken to the country** was an early part of the program at the *Portland Mennonite Mission* of Portland, Oregon, that was founded on this date. The Fresh-Air Program was followed by an organized camping experience during this decade.

1925 - **First Young People's Retreat** on the campus of Bluffton College, sponsored by the *General Conference Mennonite Church.*

Jugendvereine established by the *Mennonite Brethren* of Manitoba and Saskatchewan. Youth Fellowships had been introduced into their United States congregations earlier.

1926 - **General Conference Mennonite Youth Retreats** spread to campus of Bethel College, Newton, Kansas, and to Eastern and Pacific districts.

1927 - **First Young People's Institute** sponsored by the *Mennonite Church* on the campus of Goshen College, Goshen, Indiana.

First Youth Retreat sponsored by the *Eastern District of the General Conference Mennonites* on the grounds of University of Pennsylvania.

Youth movements within the Mennonite Church to be studied by the newly appointed Young People's Problems Committee. Literary societies and other gatherings are without churchwide direction.

Retreat for boys and girls sponsored by the *Eastern District of the General Conference Mennonite Church* near Green Lane, Pennsylvania.

1928 - **First Retreat for Youth** sponsored by the *California District of the General Conference Mennonite Church.*

Camps and Retreats Among the Hopi Indians of Arizona

Christian mission work among the Hopis was begun in 1894 by General Conference Mennonite missionaries. About this time other denominations started mission work among other Indian tribes of the Southwest. These missionaries soon felt a need for fellowship and learning from each other, since they were so far removed from their home churches. They began meeting informally in 1903 at the Mennonite Mission, Oraibi, Arizona, a Hopi village. These gatherings became an annual affair, and grew into a missionary conference. One of the main purposes of these meetings was to get Indian converts involved in the larger fellowship of believers, both Indian and white, and in Bible study and prayer. The General Conference Mennonites had a very active part in this.

By 1914 this gathering of Indian and white Christians adopted for their summer conference the name of *Southwest Bible and Missionary Conference.* That year they also purchased thirty-eight acres five miles east of Flagstaff, Arizona, in the beautiful pines at the foot of Mt. Elden. This camping movement drew large audiences. Friends of the Christian Indians were also invited, and many took part and found the Lord there. Others dedicated their lives for Christian service. Among these was a young man by the name of Theodore Epp, son of Rev. J. B. Epp, a missionary to the Hopis. Theodore Epp later founded the Back to the Bible broadcast.

By 1914 there were quite a few Christian Indian families attending these gatherings, and classes and activities were planned for all ages. This led to the beginning of youth camps at times other than the two-week Bible conference. Each mission chose a specific week in the summer for its own tribal youth. These camps were held on the same grounds as the conference because of the facilities.

In 1949 the Hopi Mennonite churches started a week of camping for their youth. This continued for some years. Later, however, in order to get the Hopi youth into the larger fellowship of Christians from all the tribes and people, they decided to get their youth involved in the two weeks of Bible Conference.

More recently, because of the larger number of Christians among the tribes of the Southwest, and since they have strong Christian leaders in their own tribes, they have started having family camps among their own people. These camps are planned by their leaders and, to a large extent, they use their native languages and their own customs for feeding and housing. Besides these localized camps there are also several Indian conferences held on the conference grounds each summer, entirely planned and conducted by Indian leaders of tribes from many places in the United States. Indians from all over America attend these gatherings.[4]

The Oregon Camping Story and the Man Behind It

Some tents, a patch of woods, a couple of old cook stoves, and some boys and girls were the only ingredients Allen Good needed to have a camping program. There were plenty of the latter living around the mission in Portland, Oregon, where he was the pastor in the early 1920s. He would bypass all the red tape and make camping simple, at least as we see it now. One of his camping sessions is described this way in his newsletter: "There were thirty boys. They slept in a large tent on a bed of straw covered with canvas. The kitchen was two cook stoves under a couple of large trees. The camp lasted ten days."

Allen Good was not the first person with the vision for getting city children into the country, and using the experience for spiritual growth and evangelism, but he was the first to introduce it into the Mennonite Church. "He was a man of great ambition and vision," said Albert and Ethel Snyder as I visited in their home about Allen Good and his camping program. They had been involved in those beginning days. "He tried many things," they continued. "Some worked, others didn't." As I tried to learn more about this person and his program, another person commented, "He had the conviction that city children should get out-of-doors, into the country, and under a Christian influence."

The first program for getting city children into the country sponsored by the church was modeled after and inspired by the Fresh Air Program in which rural families took city children into their homes several weeks during the summer. Mennonite families in the Willamette Valley of Oregon were challenged to take city children into homes on the farm. The response was good the first summer. But each summer it became more difficult to get families to take children. To Allen Good there had to be a way. That is when he took his tents and old cook stoves into the woods, and the boys and girls went along.

It was several summers before the kitchen got a roof over it. It was still longer before tents were pitched on platforms to keep them dry. Women of the surrounding congregations made comforters for the children's bedding. It had to be laundered often because it was not uncommon for children to have problems of bed-wetting. At the end of each summer the women would wash and mend the comforters and get them ready for the next summer. Surrounding congregations would provide food and other services.

As she was telling the story of those early experiences, a former staff person could laugh as she told about difficult situations. She told how some nights they would get rained out and would go to the barns at a nearby church to spend the night. One night all the campers slept on a neighbor's porch. She shared how they often asked themselves why they were doing it under such circumstances. "Why did you keep going back summer after summer?" I asked. With a chuckle, she replied, "It was something we wanted to do. We knew the values were greater than the obstacles."

Activities at the mission back in Portland included Sunday school, summer Bible school, and boys' and girls' club work. The summer camping program became an established tradition for the mission church. It was used as an incentive for attendance in other functions that were not as appealing to the boys and girls. Superintendents who served in later years kept up the program with few interruptions. Quality of accommodations improved over the years, and the staff had more conveniences. However, there is nothing to verify that improved facilities made the program more effective. Hundreds of boys and girls went through the program. The story of the Portland, Oregon, camping program has no ending. Ripple effects are still being felt from this first camping story that unfolded in the Mennonite Church.[5]

The Retreat Movement of the Twenties

An important phase of the youth movement during this period of time was the introduction of retreats for youth of high school and college age. The need for something to challenge this age group was felt throughout the churches. It was emphasized by leaders such as Austin Keiser (GC) and A. J. Metzler (MC), along with their colleagues. Many people quickly became involved in the leadership and promotion of retreats as the movement spread.

At a Christian Workers' Conference held at Bluffton, Ohio, in 1925 on the theme "Our Young People," William Weaver recalls that it was then that Austin Keiser talked about something definite that could be done. A group decided to meet in the near future and invite Vernon Smucker, representing the Mennonite Church and its young people, along with representation from the General Conference Mennonite Church. This committee planned the first nine-day retreat for August of 1925. Keiser was then a young man of twenty-eight, two years out of seminary and in his first pastorate. His burden for the youth was outstanding. Three propositions were embodied in the retreat movement as expressed by Keiser. First, the rising church wants something to do. A new day is at hand, and the youth are the ones who can make it or mar it. Secondly, the church has the key to the new day—her gospel, her history, her missions. Thirdly, the proper method of presenting this challenge remains to be found, and in young people's retreats is to be found the answer. The young people had been caught off guard in World War I. They did not know how to respond to the sudden call for decision. This must not happen again.[6]

Keiser was active in promoting the retreat movement and is credited in the *General Conference Mennonite Church* as its founder. At the 1923 Freeman, South Dakota, conference there had been considerable thinking regarding young people's work. Keiser comments, "We were thinking of the value of a young people's conference. There was quite a bit of discussion as to whether it should be called a "retreat," some thinking that it meant going backwards. We borrowed the phrase from the Roman Catholic Church as a time to draw apart and think on important problems, and so the name held."[7]

Both the *Bluffton News* and the *Witmarsum* covered the first retreat. The August 13, 1925, *Bluffton News* carried the headline, "Sixty Here for Week Retreat." The story read, "World problems of today and their solution on the basis of Christianity are being studied by sixty young people at the Mennonite Young People's Retreat which is being held on the campus of Bluffton College this week. Young men and women between the ages of eighteen and thirty years from churches in Ohio, Indiana, Illinois, Pennsylvania, and Canada are in attendance. Enrollment is more than double the number expected, and it is possible it will be made an annual affair. Afternoons are devoted to recreation. The forenoons are given to study of present-day problems including various phases of international peace, the race question and world fellowship." Since 1925, in some form and at some place, retreats have been held every year.

The beginning of the retreat movement in the *Mennonite Church* came through the Young People's Problems Committee. This committee came into being in 1921. It was to be a study committee to determine what activities there were in the church for youth, and to isolate problems that might be resulting from them. In 1927 it acquired the status of a standing committee to study existing young people's problems, and to bring them to the attention of all concerned.

Early in the 1920s the church had sent young men into the Near East in relief work assignments. When they returned to their churches and communities they were concerned with the youth and some of the situations related to them and their needs. They became involved in sharing these observations and concerns. As a result, youth conventions began showing up at various places.

Leadership was coming from the young people entirely. From 1924 to 1928 they published a paper, the *Christian Exponent*. Since these were not sponsored by a church agency, this movement was not favorably accepted by conference leaders. There were other activities among the youth without official sanction, such as the Literary Societies, which were not designed for religious instruction, but provided social and cultural events in the community.

The Young People's Problems Committee, appointed in response to such activities, isolated concerns for the church such as the desire for more and better training in the schools, leaving their home communities and going to the cities, problems related to the automobile, and the changing economic status of older members of the church. They circulated a form letter to church periodicals suggesting articles such as: "Choosing a Life Work

Now Versus a Generation Ago," "In the World, but Not of It," "The Automobile and Our Young People," and "The Young Person in This Materialistic Generation."

In 1928 a churchman wrote to Orie Miller and O. N. Johns, members of the Problems Committee, as follows: "I have also noted a strong emphasis given by the brethren on nature studies. I cannot see how such a program will fit into our rural congregations. This sectional conference idea may appeal to some of our young people, and it may be possible to conduct such conferences on a religious basis. . . . By the time this is done there will be other influences at work that must be counteracted. . . . There is danger in having something separate for a small group of believers within the church. This is a departure from the common practice in all our church activities." He remarked that the Sunday school and the Young People's Bible meetings had always been shared by the entire church and all ages.[8]

Orie Miller replied by stating that at that time young people were coming into the church between the ages of twelve and fifteen, but between the ages of sixteen and twenty-five large numbers were leaving. He stated, "This problem needs to be brought to the attention of all church leaders. This 16-25 age group is the one we are concerned about as a Committee." A resolution in 1929 recognized the Christian Life Conferences. There was a note of caution, however. The resolution read: "We believe the Christian Life Conference can be a great service to our young people if properly supervised. We further believe that the aim of each conference should contribute to the deepening of the spiritual life of our young people of the church."

The Problems Committee sponsored a Young People's Institute on the Goshen College campus, Goshen, Indiana, in 1927. Although the youth were not involved in the planning, they had influenced decisions that led up to the institute. They were receptive to the idea, and supported it with enthusiasm. This was not only a first for the church, but the beginning of a new relationship for young people and the adult membership of the church.

The youth movement among the *Mennonite Brethren* during this time was also undergoing the changes characteristic of the time. J. A. Toews, church historian, noted, "In the first two decades of the twentieth century youth fellowship groups became generally accepted in the Mennonite Brethren churches of Russia. It should be noted, however, that there was a separate organization for the young men, and the young women. These fellowship meetings were not only attended by members of the church, but also by unsaved relatives and friends of members. The purpose of these meetings was to promote spiritual growth of believers, and to influence the unsaved to make a personal commitment to Christ."[9]

As the Mennonite Brethren emigrated from Russia they brought the youth movement with them. By the mid-twenties the *Jugendverein* was an established institution in the early Mennonite Brethren churches of Manitoba and Saskatchewan, but it was influenced by patterns set in the United States. This was understandable since the churches in Manitoba had been founded through the evangelistic outreach of the brethren from the south, and the first churches in Saskatchewan were established by immigrants from Minnesota, Nebraska, North Dakota, and other states.[10]

In the late twenties the *Jugendverein* was undergoing gradual transformation. It was no longer a ministry for the youth, but a ministry by the youth. There also appeared a shift in emphasis from mutual fellowship to public service. As Allen Peters observed: "The *Jugendverein* developed into a periodic Sunday evening service for the benefit of the entire church, where youth presented a program of general interest to the entire church.[11]

The retreats of the General Conference Mennonites; the Young People's institutes of the Mennonite Church; and the *Jugendvereine* (youth fellowships) of the Mennonite Brethren had much in common, and all were in the interests of the youth. They provided an opportunity for youth to become a part of the church and for church leaders and youth to interact. Youth began to see their leaders as real people, and church leaders began to see their youth in a new way. At these gatherings they ate together, worked together, worshiped together, and played together. It was a relationship that could not be duplicated in the conventional church structure.

Edith Herr, one of the camping pioneers, reflects the experience of many when she says, "It was at these young people's Institutes that I got to know some of our church leaders." She elaborated on her appreciation of this, and the values it had in influencing her as a young Christian.[12] This, no doubt, was one of the unexpected values that came out of the retreat movement of the twenties.

CHAPTER THREE

The Thirties

A Decade of Dreams

The Thirties was the decade
when seeds began to take root
that would result in a chain of camps
and retreat centers
wherever there was a
concentration of Mennonite churches.

The thirties were years of following dreams and blazing new trails that would result in a chain of camps and retreat centers across America wherever there was a concentration of Mennonite churches. God was working in the lives of many people to bring this about. Visions of this outdoor ministry were all different, and yet the nurture and evangelism of youth and children was always the ultimate goal. Sometimes it was the Sunday school that spawned the idea, and the program was tailored to strengthen the program of the church and its families. In other instances it was the pastors and city mission workers who had a concern for the city children, and saw the outdoor ministry as a way of meeting some of their needs. They saw it as a way to supplement their Sunday school and summer Bible school programs. Other church leaders had a concern for the youth in the church and felt something must be done to challenge them to discipleship and loyalty to the church and its traditions.

In Saskatchewan Henry Janzen and others shared a concern for the children of the community who were not receiving religious instruction, as well as the children of their own homes. They did not wait for the development of facilities, but for several years used leased and improvised facilities to make their ministry possible. It was in the forties before Elim Gospel Beach became their base of operation.

The scene for youth retreats of the Colorado Mennonite churches was the Colorado Rockies. As early as 1935 the youth of the area took their summer retreat to Manitou Springs, Colorado, and utilized the outdoor setting. Using the local church as their base, they went into various scenic areas for afternoon and evening events.

In southwestern Pennsylvania a movement was on foot to provide a twelve-day young people's institute to replace the traditional five-day events being held on college campuses and at congregations. The vision included the idea for a setting in an outdoor environment. The popular Arbutus Park Institute near Johnstown, Pennsylvania, continued for seven years and was partly responsible for the securing of a permanent retreat center, now known as Laurelville Mennonite Church Center.

In eastern Pennsylvania the General Conference Mennonites were dreaming of a church-owned campsite to strengthen their existing program of young people's retreats and camps for boys and girls. Their inspiration and dialogue came out of their Christian Endeavor conventions. Camp Men-O-Lan was the result.

In the woodlot on an Oregon farm, Glenn Whitaker, newly appointed pastor of the Portland, Oregon, mission, improvised facilities for several weeks of summer camp for boys and girls from the city. Facilities were simple with only the basics provided. The program was staffed by volunteer workers, with the people of the surrounding churches providing food and other services.

Holiness camps and camp meetings emerged in the Brethren in Christ churches in this decade. The first camp developed from a series of annual evangelistic meetings begun in the 1930s on the outskirts of the small town of Roxsbury, Pennsylvania. Carlton O. Wittlinger in *Quest for Piety and Obedience* says, "In some respects tent meetings and Bible conferences were forerunners of the holiness camps, but the latter were unique in making holiness doctrine and experience the unifying emphasis of the services and related activities. These were not only camp meetings, but holiness camp meetings."

Many of the youth gatherings of this time were not designed as an outdoor ministry, but were held wherever the meeting could be arranged. Moving them to a setting with an outdoor atmosphere came about gradually. Camps for boys and girls were thought of as an outreach to unchurched children as well as for children from the church. Youth gatherings were often tailored for youth already in the church. There was caution regarding leadership, and the gatherings were usually denominationally oriented. One program of that time read, "Participants are to be ages 15-27 and brothers and sisters who are communicant members of their respective congregations."

A letter from one of the youth leaders, Orie Miller, to Paul Mininger in 1934 states his concern, "Our young people are in need of help; and in most communities are not getting it. They need help in meeting perplexing problems and temptations of the modern world." He further suggests that the church is not meeting these needs through existing programs such as the Sunday school and institutes. He expresses concern about the quality of spiritual life young people are experiencing. "They just get by with frequent confessions." He observes that these conditions do not exist in the same proportion where Bible schools are available.[1]

There was evidence of concern among other Mennonite groups. S. F. Pannabecker, General Conference Mennonite historian, comments about this decade as follows, "Coming to the thirties it is easy to detect a growing interest and participation on the part of the young people in church activities. A section of *The Mennonite* is again devoted to young people's interests after having been dropped. A. R. Keiser is the editor of the column. Problems are discussed such as education, vocation, finding a partner. They air their views on what they expect of the church, and what they can do for the church."

As the curtain dropped on the 1930s, camping for boys and girls and retreats and institutes for young people had found its way into eight states and three provinces of Canada. The movement included the states of Oregon, California, and Arizona to the west, and as far east as Pennsylvania. Central states included Kansas, Colorado, Indiana, and Ohio. The provinces of Saskatchewan, Manitoba, and Ontario had seen either camping for boys and girls or retreats and institutes during this decade.

Meanwhile, in the social and political arena of society at large, events were developing that would both affect the life and thought of the church and the development of camping in the next decade. It was the decade of the great depression. In some parts of the country it was the time of prolonged drought, dust storms, and grasshoppers. For many families poverty was the accepted way of life. Hitler rose to power in Germany and sent his troops into the Rhineland. President Roosevelt condemned the Hitler outbreak, and the stage was set for World War II.

Significant Events in the 1930s

1930 - **Three Young People's Institutes** were sponsored by the *Mennonite Church* at Goshen, Indiana, Scottdale, Pennsylvania and Kitchener, Ontario.
Holiness Camp Meeting at Roxsbury, Pennsylvania; a first by the *Brethren in Christ*.
Camping program for children started by the *Mennonite Brethren Church* on the shores of Lake Winnipeg. Definite dates not known.

1933 - **Churchwide youth program** established by the *Mennonite Brethren Church*.
Young People's Institute sponsored by *Mennonite Church* at Hesston, Kansas, with 300 in attendance.

1935 - **Young People's Institute** sponsored by the *Mennonite Churches* of Colorado take their activities to the Colorado Rockies at Manitou Springs.
Roxsbury Holiness Camp, Roxsbury, Pennsylvania, sponsored by the *Brethren in Christ* develops permanent facilities.
Churchwide Young People's Retreat, a first for the *General Conference Mennonite Church* at Camp LaVerne in California.

1936 - **Arbutus Park Twelve-Day Institute** sponsored by the *Mennonite Church* holds its first season near Johnstown, Pennsylvania, and continued for several summers.

MENNONITE CAMPING PROGRAMS BEGUN IN THE 1930

This map shows the approximate location of the 12
camping and retreat programs begun in the 1930s
Beginning dates and names are shown in the
chronological listing for the 1930s

■ Permanent facilities
○ Improvised or leased facilities

1937 - **The purchase of land** for developing their retreat program was discussed in a conference session at East Swamp, Pennsylvania, by the Eastern District of the *General Conference Mennonite Church.* J. Walter Landis offered his farm. This was possibly the first land secured for the express purpose of developing a retreat ground.

Christian Leader, established by the *Mennonite Brethren Youth Committee*; the first conference periodical in the English language dedicated to the interests of the young people. In 1951 it becomes the official English organ of the *Mennonite Brethren Conference.*

Portland, Oregon, youth camping program that began in the early twenties and sponsored by the *Mennonite Church* has new director, Glenn Whitaker.

1938 - **Camp Men-O-Lan developed** by the Eastern District of the *General Conference Mennonite Church* near Quakertown, Pennsylvania.

First Youth Retreat sponsored by the Southern District of the *Mennonite Brethren* for all the youth of their district, held on the campus of Phillips University, Enid, Oklahoma. Continued for several years.

1939 - **Camp Arroyo Sico** founded by the *Calvary Mennonite Church,* Los Angeles, California, under the leadership of Glenn Whitaker, newly appointed pastor. This improvised facility preceded Hidden Valley Camp established later.

Mennonite Brethren in the 1930s

Mennonite Brethren camping activity on the shore of Lake Winnipeg dates back to the 1930s. At that time it was under the direction of Winkler Bible School, which annually rented the Canadian Sunday School Mission grounds at Gimli and conducted a camp based on a Sunday school teacher training format. However, a drawback was that the CSSM needed the facilities for its own summer programs, so the only time available for Winkler Bible School was before these programs got under way. This meant the WBS program had to be held quite early, which from the standpoint of weather was not satisfactory. Two or three years later the school rented the Gimli property, supplied its own cook, director, and other requirements, and operated its own camp.

The Bible school staff was active in the camp. Rev. A. H. Unruh, Bible school president and Rev. J. G. Wiens, vice-president, both taught at the camp. Rev. A. A. Kroeker, secretary-treasurer of WBS, served as manager. Campers paid little in the way of fees.

They would bring whatever supplies they could from the farm, such as ham, eggs, butter, sausage, and the like. The cook, usually a farm girl from the Winkler area, would work without pay. So, the overhead was quite low.

Mr. Kroeker recalls: "We were always looking out for property to buy as our own so we wouldn't need to hold our camps so early. Then one day in 1939 I was in the drugstore in Gimli and I met an old gentleman, Mr. H. P. Tergeson, an Icelander. We struck up a conversation and I mentioned our problem to him. He said to me, 'I hef a vunderful place. It is on the lake, and for dat purpose I vould sell it.' "

Mr. Kroeker then organized a group of ten men from Winkler, Morden, and Winnipeg, and they drove out one day to see Mr. Tergeson's property, located some seventy miles north of Winnipeg. They drove past the property—there was no access road then—until they came to the Arnes road. They drove to the end of it and walked back along the beach until they came to Mr. Tergeson's land. There was plenty of beachfront then, more than enough so they could walk all the way without getting their feet wet.

When they arrived at the site, Mr. Tergeson let out a wistful sigh and said, "I always knew it vus goot, but I neffer knew it vus so goot." There it was, 160 acres of beautiful beachfront property, with a large clearing. Many years earlier it had been a farmstead, and all that remained of the original habitation was a trace of the concrete foundation.

The price was $1,000.

"It really was a beautiful beach at the time," recalls Mr. Kroeker. "We walked back to where the cars were and I don't think we talked more than two or three minutes before we made up our minds. Everyone had already decided that it was a bargain." The ten men contributed $100 each and bought the property.

Very little work was done on the site that year. The only actual improvement was the construction of a well, located where the original dining hall was to be built later. This well served the camp many years. Plans for the development of this original camp were disrupted by the the Second World War.[2]

J. Walter Landis and Camp Men-O-Lan

The story of J. Walter Landis is seldom told without a beginning something like this: "At the age of four he suffered a leg injury which left him crippled for life." In spite of his handicap which left him on crutches, Landis remained cheerful and congenial. He possessed a faith that was contagious. Stories of Men-O-

Lan always pay tribute to this man with a vision.

The idea of a campground for the Eastern District of the General Conference Mennonite Church was ten years developing. In 1928 the conference had sponsored their first annual young people's retreat. At that time the leaders of the movement began thinking about their own campground. In 1937 at the Sunday School Union Convention there was discussion from the floor regarding the purchase of property for this purpose. J. Walter Landis saw his opportunity to bring his dream for a Sunday school playground into reality. He offered to donate his property if it was suitable. A retreat ground became reality.

In 1981 Men-O-Lan celebrated its fortieth anniversary. In a history written for the occasion there was a section entitled, "I remember when" where observations out of the past were shared. Many of these tell the Walter Landis story at its best.

"I remember when," says Emily Shaffer, "Walter Landis came to visit my parents on the farm and said he had purchased a farm, and that he hoped to see it one day become a camp especially for the Eastern District Conference with a special outreach to city children. We all thought it was just another of Walter's dreams."

"He had a dream of a community Sunday school playground," recalls James Gerhart, one of his Sunday school pupils. "He bought the Jona Scheetz farm at the tax sale for $1,700. He asked the young people of his 'Victor' class to help him develop it into a Sunday school playground. We did not share his vision, and always there were no finances."

"I remember when," observes Olin Krehbiel, "I met Walter to look over his land. He, on crutches, and I walked amidst trees, streams, and clearings as he showed me several plots in his total farm acreage."

Herb Fretz remembered, "He would come many afternoons with his crutches and would sit on a big rock under the trees, watching as we played softball or as the smaller children played about. I can still see the smile on his face and sense of peace and contentment that he had given something out of his own life which was now helping hundreds of children and young people to find joy in Christian camping and in the Lord. I would often go and sit with him awhile and talk."

Years before when the discussion on the conference floor concerned a church-owned campground, not everyone shared in the vision. A number argued that the church had no business or need going into the woods with all the snakes, rocks, and thorns to begin a camp. When God has a plan God puts the dream into someone's heart. God probably chooses those who have a faith to live by, a conscience to live with, and a purpose to live for.[3]

Going Camping with Glenn Whitaker

To know Glenn Whitaker was to know a man with a dream and the drive to see that it happened. His career in camping started in 1937, while superintendent of the Mennonite Mission at Portland, Oregon, and came to an unfortunate end in 1945 due to broken health. By that time he had developed the first permanent campsite in the Mennonite Church, known as Hidden Valley, located near Los Angeles, California. He had revived the camping ministry of the Portland, Oregon, Mennonite Mission in Oregon, and developed a camping ministry known as Arroyo Sico as part of his ministry to boys and girls near Los Angeles where he was pastoring the Calvary Mennonite Church.

Wherever Glenn was pastor there was the Sunday school, the Summer Bible school, clubs for boys and girls, and summer camps. When he assumed leadership at the Portland, Oregon, Mennonite Mission he became involved in all of these. His concern is best illustrated by his own words in the *Portland Mission Newsletter*, 1937:

> For some time we have been burdened with the problem of how to keep the junior boys and girls in our Sunday school. One of the disappointments in city mission work is to see boys and girls drop out of Sunday school just about the time they are old enough to make a decision for Christ.

Summer camp could be the answer. That is what he found it to be. It provided the bridge which many boys and girls crossed in their pilgrimage of the Christian life and fellowship in the church. During Glenn's first summer he wrote in *Portland Mission Newsletter*:

> The very next day after the close of Bible school the tents and other camping equipment were loaded into the truck and trailer and taken to the country where the camp would be located. It was late that night when a small group of men started back to Portland. They had left behind them a little village of tents hid away in a beautiful grove of fir. This was on Saturday. Mission meeting was held on Monday, and Tuesday the first group was taken to camp.

The camp was on the Sam Miller farm. Sam had donated lumber to build a kitchen, ten by twelve feet. Seven new tents were purchased to add to the equipment that had accumulated over the years. The season provided two sessions for boys and two for girls, all from the city. Each camp was ten days in length, with a fee of two dollars per camper. Congregations of the area assisted with food and other services. After two years of ministry at Portland, Glenn was transferred to Los Angeles, California, but he left a tradition and model for Christian camping that was followed by others.

Glenn's arrival at the Calvary Mennonite Church in Los Angeles resulted in a growing Sunday school and an active program for boys and girls of the community. When the Sunday school grew too large for their building, he got permission from the city to pitch a tent for classes. When that was filled, the garage and parsonage were used. The program would not be complete without a summer camp.

Arroyo Sico was the name and location chosen for the first summer camp. It was a government-owned campground, reserved for groups, and equipped with tables and stoves. The church got together other minimal equipment. In some cases campers even brought their own tents.

Glenn's camping programs were packed with Bible study. Each morning he put his campers through a pace of six classes, one each twenty minutes. Each camper had a mimeographed book with lesson outlines. They took their books and went from class to class in rapid succession. Glenn said this kept it from getting monotonous.

"Glenn was an ingenious organizer and planner," his wife, Ferne, told me in an interview about their camping experiences. "He could think of things to add interest. He had his own camp currency. Campers would be paid in this currency for doing camp chores. Then they would make homemade ice cream, and campers would purchase it with their camp currency. Campers could learn to flip their own pancakes. First they used a practice pancake. When they had mastered the art they flipped their own up into the air and back into the skillet."

His techniques were effective. Two campers were so enthusiastic about their Bible classes and camping experience that when they returned to their homes in the city they took over the family garage, set up a vacation Bible school, recruited children from up and down the street, and used these same materials for their Bible school.

In 1942 the Calvary Mennonite Church in Los Angeles purchased a small acreage in the mountains near Los Angeles. The camp, given the name Hidden Valley, was located in the scenic Pacoima Canyon, bordered by a mountain stream and surrounded with steep mountain cliffs. It was equipped with cabins and tent houses for sleeping quarters. Other buildings were a dining hall and kitchen, and an infirmary. It was originally built for twenty campers, but was expanded each year. Tents were on frames and beds were equipped with springs and mattresses.

Camping was simple in those days. The basics were all that were required or necessary. Campers carried all of their water from the spring. Food preparation was shared by all the campers. The campers were not only living in an outdoor setting, they were relating to it, seeing themselves as a part of God's creation, and experiencing God's presence and working in all of creation, including themselves.

The Whitakers purchased land adjacent to the campsite to make room for a swimming pool. Glenn felt this was important to the program. In his characteristic way he did not ask for funding in the usual way. People supporting camping with their purses were few and far between in those days. These were the depression years, and people with ingenuity found out that a lot of things could happen without a lot of money. Glenn, with the help of others, dug the pool by hand. It was about four feet deep on the average. All the cement was mixed with a hand mixer, and rocks were carried from the stream to put into the cement to make it go a bit farther. It was large enough for swimming, and a small boat could be used in it.

"We are now more convinced than ever that summer camp work is one of the most effective ways of winning the city boys and girls to Christ. We do not need handwork in the classes to keep them interested. Just being in camp made it interesting enough, and the six classes each morning could be solid teaching." Glenn reported his feelings about camp in this way in an article in the *Gospel Herald*, 1941. Many decisions for Christ were made at each camp session, although his evangelistic appeal was low key, and the campers, he says, came to staff.

Glenn's faith and perseverance was contagious. It was caught, not taught. When the foxes were getting into the cookies at night, the Whitakers' young son Warren came up with the solution. "We'll ask God to keep the foxes out of the cookies." A trailer pulled behind the family car was the only transportation from the city to the camp for hauling supplies. Glenn needed a station wagon, so he started to pray about it. One of his summer campers said, "The Lord gives you everything else you ask for, but we'll have to see about this one." When the station wagon arrived, the boy's faith grew.

Broken health ended Glenn Whitaker's active camping career in 1945. He had sown seeds and pioneered in a ministry that continued in many ways. The Calvary Mennonite Church did not choose to continue the program at Hidden Valley and it was sold. However, they continued the camping ministry as part of their program. Glenn had made his contribution in making Christian camping a tradition in the Mennonite churches of Oregon and

California. God gave him many useful years of ministry in other ways, and he retired to his home in Pueblo, Colorado, where he lived for many years.[4]

The Laurelville Story

Allen Good in Oregon, Glenn Whitaker in California, Henry Janzen in Saskatchewan, and others involved in mission programs, were concerned with meeting spiritual needs of children. They improvised facilities which included only the basics. They did not wait for organization and buildings. At this same time A. J. Metzler and his colleagues had dreams of a different sort. They dreamed of a church center that could provide opportunity for all age groups and various functions.

In the summer of 1923 the biennial general conference of the Mennonite Church gave serious attention to the need for nurturing the large number of young people in the church. This conference created a group labeled Young People's Problems Committee with Orie O. Miller, an unordained young businessman from Akron, Pennsylvania, as chairman. The committee sponsored meetings which came to be known as Young People's Institutes. For seven years, institutes of four to five days were successfully conducted. In 1934 the Southwestern Pennsylvania Conference appointed a committee of three (A. J. Metzler, C. F. Yake, and Ezra C. Bender) with assignment to sponsor a conference institute. This committee carried out a successful twelve-day Young People's Institute at Arbutus Park. The publicity folder for the 1936 institute, written by C. F. Yake, began: "Youth faces a vacation problem today such as the young people of a generation ago knew nothing about. Worldly progress has been made with tremendous strides during the past decade, especially so in travel and communication. With this progress has come the development and commercialization of natural resorts as public playgrounds, providing in most instances attractions and worldly amusements that are extremely demoralizing. Intensely appealing advertisements are drawing many of our young people to places represented as wholesome and uplifting, while frequently forces of evil are crouching behind in the shadows. . . . To provide better for the vacation needs of our young people this twelve-day institute has been conceived in prayer and planned and developed through much counseling and sacrifical labor."

Two years later an unequivocal call for the establishment of a church camp was voiced by A. J. Metzler in the July 21, 1938, *Gospel Herald.* The first paragraph included a call to action: "During the past years the Mennonite Church has always been awake to the needs and problems of its constituency. She has been zealous for finding the best possible solutions for needs and problems as they arise. We are grateful, not only to the Lord for His direction in the past, but also to the men of vision and conviction whom He used in meeting these needs with scriptural and practical solutions."

In the founding of Laurelville three men stand out as prominent in the develpment of the camp and its program: A. J. Metzler, C. F. Yake, and Orie O. Miller. As early as 1935 these men were busy promoting the idea of a church camp and trying to find a site for such a facility. They were also getting recruits. As the group increased in number they referred to themselves as the "prospectors."

Finding Laurelville is an exciting story showing God's leading and timing as a dream became reality. Wenger tells it this way in his history: "Late in the summer of 1942, a brother in the Scottdale congregation came to A. J. Metzler's office and gave him a startling bit of information. A church camp was for sale—within twelve miles of Scottdale! The one who gave the report was David S. Brilhart and the place he referred to was the Methodist camp along Jacobs Creek about four miles east of Mount Pleasant. This news literally took A. J. Metzler's breath away, as he now reports the incident. For almost ten years he had been driving east on Route 31 to look at possible camp locations, all of which proved to be unsuitable. All the while he was driving right past the place which met every conceivable criterion that the prospecting committee had drawn up over the years of search. . . . The purchase price was $12,000. . . . The group agreed 'tentatively' to take the camp. . . . Pledges totaled $7,000. . . . The swimming pool was a disconcerting factor. The minutes reveal agreement in these words: 'since the pool is already on the grounds it shall be preserved as part of the camp, but enclosed.' . . . On October 13, 1943, Laurelville Camp came into being."[5]

CHAPTER FOUR

The Forties

A Decade of Growth

The Forties was a time of
phenomenal growth in camps and retreats
among the Mennonite conferences
as compared to previous decades.
It was a new era for youth within the churches;
the beginning of rapid expansion
for camp development.

The expansion of this outdoor ministry in the decade of the 1940s was phenomenal as compared to previous decades. Nineteen additional camps and retreat centers had been established by the end of the decade and numerous youth camping programs were serving children across the United States and Canada using leased and improvised facilities. Retreats and institutes for young people grew in popularity and moved from the formal settings of congregations and college campuses to informal settings with an outdoor atmosphere.

Experiences and success out of the past were causing people to think in terms of owning and operating their own facilities. This seemed to be a consuming desire among many leaders of that time. Leased facilities were not conducive for growth. Available dates were limited and often unsuitable. This left no opportunity for expanding the program to include other ages and interests. Those who had the vision and who provided leadership were daring and determined, and the stories of some of these beginnings are accounts of modern miracles. The camping movement experienced rapid growth, so that today the Mennonite churches probably hold some kind of per capita record for the number of camps and retreat centers.

During this decade there was little or no sharing between the leaders of these scattered programs. Each group was left up to its own ingenuity and resourcefulness. In a few cases conference bodies gave support to development and program. Young people's organizations were responsible for the purchase and development of others. In other instances there were small interest groups who formed associations or societies to develop facilities and program. And, in some instances, individuals with limited support from their churches followed their personal dreams and established programs that later became established camps or retreat centers.

Program trends followed those of previous decades. Those involved in church planting were quick to see the value of the camping ministry for outreach and evangelism and their programs were designed to meet this need. Those whose background was retreats and institutes were programming primarily for the youth within the churches, and with few exceptions were not thinking in terms of outreach. There were others who were concerned with the plight of inner city children, or children with physical and emotional handicaps. Vacationing trends in a changing society were the concern of another group, and they saw the development of campsites as a solution for Christians' vacations. In spite of this wide scope of rationale behind the movement, there were many common features. Programs were

Bible centered and evangelistic, often taking on the form of Bible conferences, with recreation included. Outdoor camping skills and nature-oriented activities were not usually included as a part of the program at this stage.

This was the decade of World War II which disrupted and changed the lives and circumstances of so many. Events in this decade shook the foundations of the churches, homes, and the minds of the church leaders. Conscription and issues of peace surfaced, and the questions they created could not be swept under the rug. There were decisions to make that had not been necessary previously. Many discovered they were not prepared for these decisions, nor to cope with some of the new circumstances thrust upon them. Suddenly there were more questions than answers.

This was not all bad. It created cause for dialogue and searching. Civilian Public Service Camps were established in the United States for conscientious objectors. Young people, both men and women, were deeply affected by this program as they moved from the security of their communities into cities and jobs that were foreign to them. This has no doubt had a greater impact on the movement of camping and retreats than is recognized. All at once the church was scattered. People were uprooted from their traditional rural communities to urban settings. New ideas and convictions surfaced and movements and trends in the churches were often affected in a positive way.

It was also a new era for youth within the Mennonite conferences. Positive trends were established that have continued. Youth were included in the mainstream of the church. Organized youth teams traveled from community to community to organize and encourage local youth groups. Some communities were sponsoring youth revivals. There were numerous opportunities provided for leadership training.

Paul Erb, an outstanding leader in the youth movement of that time, reported to the Commission for Christian Education in the Mennonite Church in 1948, "The outstanding happening for the young people of the Mennonite Church was the endorsement at the general conference of the plan for the organization of the Mennonite Youth Fellowship. . . . A meeting with young people indicated marked interest of the youth in this movement, and also in giving it a strong spiritual emphasis." With this action, the youth of the Mennonite Church moved into a new role. They were involved in the program of the church, and accepting responsibility in leadership and planning.

J. A. Toews comments on the status of the Mennonite Brethren youth movement during this period as follows: "Several factors contributed to the widespread interest in Christian camping among Mennonite Brethren following World War II. Rapid urbanization, growing affluence, a concern for the physical, social, and spiritual welfare of children and young people. These gave an impetus to the establishment of summer camps throughout the country. Perhaps because of the brief summer season, the Mennonite Brethren in the prairie provinces pioneered in this work."

The Brethren in Christ were also experiencing growth in the camping movement during the 1940s. The motivation stemmed from holiness camp meetings, and they were active in establishing facilities and camp meetings in various locations in the United States and Canada. Roxsbury Holiness Camp had been established in Pennsylvania in the late 1930s. By the late forties the holiness camp meeting movement had spread into Ohio and Kansas.

By this date in history the American Camping Association reported that an estimated 20,000 churches of all denominations were involved in some form of Christian camping. A similar trend existed in Canada. Some of these churches had become involved as early as the turn of the century. Christian camping was experiencing rapid growth, and was becoming a significant part of the total camping movement in America.

Significant Beginnings in the 1940s

1940 - **North Carolina Youth Retreat** established with facilities and program by *Mennonite Brethren* sometime in the early 1940s. Exact date not documented. Sponsored by North Carolina District.

Oregon Youth Camps established program, using leased facilities, sponsored by *General Conference Mennonite Church*. Exact dates not documented.

Youth camps for boys and girls sponsored by *Mennonite Church* in the Peoria, Illinois, area, using leased facilities.

Statewide Young People's Institute sponsored by *Ohio Mennonite churches*, using leased facilities of Camp Siebering. Continued several years.

Niagara Holiness Camp located at Niagara Christian College, Ontario. Operates summer only. Tabernacle seats 1,000. Sponsored by *Brethren in Christ.*

1941 - **Camp Men-O-Lan** founded at Quakertown, Pennsylvania, by Eastern District of the *General Conference Mennonite Church.* First church-owned campsite in General Conference.

Canadian Holiness Camp sponsored by *Brethren in Christ*. The first for Canada.

1942 - **Hidden Valley Camp** established by the *Calvary Mennonite Church*, Los Angeles, California. First church-owned facility in the *Mennonite Church*.

First youth camp sponsored by the *Mennonite Brethren* of the Pacific District, using leased facilities at Sequoia Lake, California.

Youth Retreats organized on a conference level sometime in the early forties. No date documented. Sponsored by the Southern District of the *Mennonite Brethren*.

1943 - **Oklahoma Mennonite Retreat Grounds** established by the *General Conference Mennonite Church*, Hydro, Oklahoma.

Laurelville Mennonite Camp (now Laurelville Mennonite Church Center) founded by an association of interested parties in the *Mennonite Church*.

Memorial Holiness Camp established by the *Brethren in Christ* at Troy, Ohio. Sponsor holiness meetings and lease facilities to others.

1944 - **Mennonite Youth Fellowship** hold their first annual conference at Camp Emmaus in Illinois. Sponsored by *Mennonite Church*.

Young People's Institute sponsored by the *Iowa Mennonite Churches (MC)* at the East Union congregation, Kalona, Iowa.

West Bank Bible Camp founded by the *Mennonite Brethren* in Saskatchewan.

Mennonite Youth Farm Bible Camp founded by the *Conference of Mennonites of Saskatchewan (GC)*.

Little Eden Camp, Onekama, Michigan, founded by an association of interested persons in the *Mennonite Church*.

1945 - **Camps and retreats** sponsored by the *Mennonite Brethren* of the Pacific District with improvised facilities at General Grant Park in California. Five weeks for youth and adults.

Camp Elim, Saskatchewan, purchased by the *General Conference Mennonite Church*. Camping activities for children and youth go back to the 1930s, using leased and improvised facilities.

First annual retreats for children sponsored by the Western District of the *General Conference Mennonite Church*.

Youth Camps sponsored by the *Mennonite Mission (MC)*

at Culp, Arkansas. Camps were held for several years at Blanchard Springs State Park.

Youth retreats sponsored by the *Mennonite churches of Idaho (MC)*. Continued for a number of years, using leased and improvised facilities.

1946 - **Hartland Christian Camp**, Badger, California, founded by the *Mennonite Brethren*.

1947 - **Colorado Mountain Retreat** sponsored by the *Youth Fellowship of the Colorado Mennonite Churches (MC)*, using leased facilities at Pueblo State Park; serving youth of Colorado and surrounding states.

Camp Ebenezer, Ohio, operated by the *Mennonite Church*, using improvised facilities, serving black children from the city.

1948 - **Camp Arnes**, Winnipeg, Manitoba, founded by the *Mennonite Brethren*. Sponsored by the Lake Winnipeg Mission Camp Society.

Camp Assiniboia, Manitoba, established by *Conference of Mennonites in Manitoba (GC)*.

Indian Mennonite Retreat sponsored by the *General Conference of Mennonites of Oklahoma (GC)*.

Chesley Lake Camp, Ontario, founded by an association of interested persons within the *Mennonite Church*.

First Young People's Retreat sponsored by the Northern District of the *General Conference Mennonite Church*, using leased facilities.

Mennonite Youth of British Columbia, *(GC)*, organize for fellowship. This is the beginning of the movement resulting in Camp Squeah.

1949 - **Youth camps for mission children** began on this approximate date in the Franconia Mennonite Conference (MC), sponsored by the *Allentown Mennonite Mission*.

Mennonite Youth Village, Michigan, was established by the *Mennonite Board of Missions (MC)*, for service to underprivileged and homeless youth.

Camp Mennoscah, Kansas, established by the *General Conference Mennonite Church*.

Winkler Bible Camp, Manitoba, established by the *Mennonite Brethren*.

Camp Rehoboth, Illinois, founded by James Lark, pastor of the *Bethel Mennonite Church (MC)*, in Chicago as an outreach and ministry to city children. Now operates as a day camp sponsored by the Rehoboth Mennonite Church.

Kenbrook Bible Camp, Pennsylvania, founded by the *Brethren in Christ* as an opportunity for child evangelism.

MENNONITE CAMPING PROGRAMS BEGUN IN THE 1940s

This map shows the approximate location of the 31
camping and retreat programs begun in the 1940s
Beginning dates and names are shown in the
chronological listing for the 1940s

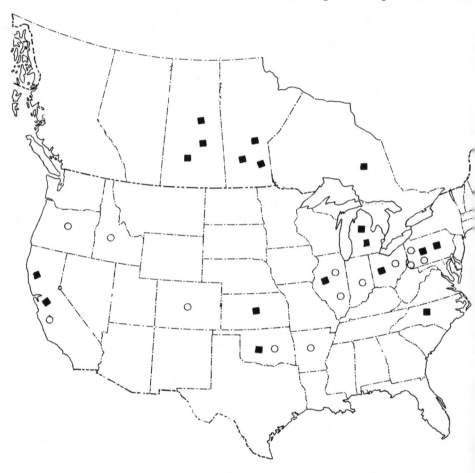

■ Permanent facilities
O Improvised or leased facilities

Camp Elim and the Henry Janzen Story

"Every nook and corner was full of campers," Henry Janzen commented when asked how many attended Camp Elim each week. "There were 150 to 200 of them. At first we put straw down for them to sleep on. Later we got mattresses, and built more cabins. The boys were in one big dormitory. They caused some trouble. The bathroom facilities created a problem. We had no running water. The people brought in a lot of the food from their homes."

The story starts in the mid-thirties, even though Camp Elim was not founded until 1945. The Mennonite congregations in the area of Swift Current, Saskatchewan, had experienced revival in the mid-thirties when a visiting evangelist was preaching in their community. This led to a concern for the people in the surrounding villages, and especially the children from other ethnic groups who were receiving no religious instruction.

Prior to the purchase of Elim Gospel Beach the summer camps for children were held at various locations in leased and improvised facilities. Records and information on these are limited. Facilities were simple, but the programs were effective, as evidenced by their continuation and growth.

Those who have known Henry Janzen speak fondly of him. He was associated with the Elim Bible Institute where he worked during the winter months, giving his summers to Christian camping. He is described as s storyteller, and evidently was good at it, whether the story was about himself or someone else.

Developing program and bringing boys and girls to camp seemed to take precedence over spending resources on buildings and equipment, as far as Henry was concerned. At least there were no frills in his camp in those early days at Elim. As the story unfolds it is clear that he had ingenuity and imagination to supplement his hard work and long hours. When the property was purchased, it included an abandoned dance hall, seven cabins, some boats and a boathouse, an icehouse, a storage building, and some farm buildings. The dance hall was converted into the dining hall, kitchen, and the tabernacle. Elim's setting is on the north shore of Lac Pelletier, located in a deep valley. It consists of a half section of prairie, a clear blue lake, and 500 poplar trees, and a half-mile of lakefront.

Students from Elim Bible Institute helped in the summer program. Since there was no running water, all water was carried from the pump by campers and staff. Since there was no refrigeration, ice was cut from the lake each winter and packed in sawdust in the icehouse. They would employ local people to put up their supply of ice each winter. However, one winter no help was available. This did not pose an impossible situation for Henry and his associates. They traveled in the dead of winter to the camp to fill the icehouse. The first twenty miles were by train. Then a farmer loaned them horses and a bobsled and they traveled the last fifty miles by bobsled to the camp. Within a couple of days they had filled the icehouse, and returned home.

When Henry was asked about finances for the camp he said, "Money was secured by donations. In the beginning the camp was purchased without any grant from the government or the church. There were six or eight of us, and we each pitched in with one hundred dollars to get it started. In the summer we operated a store for the people on the lake. Some days we would take in as much as a thousand dollars. One Sunday afternoon we sold forty-five gallons of ice cream. We rented lakefront for people to build cabins. We collected rent on as many as forty of these. It worked well. We never had any difficulty. Each spring people would come from the churches and clean up the beach, and get things ready for summer. Sometimes as many as fifty would come. They would bring wagons and tractors and stay all day. They would do carpenter work, build cabins, and often provide the materials."

When asked about program he said, "The main purpose for getting the camp was to have something for the children and the youth, as well as the surrounding community. We had services in the evenings with guest speakers. The hall was usually full. With a loudspeaker on the roof people could hear two or three miles away across the lake. Sunday afternoons we would have a choir and a guest speaker."

He recalls the story about one of their speakers who took a boat ride with some others. He was wearing his best suit. They took a watermelon along to eat while out on the lake. Something happened, and the boat capsized and dumped everyone into the water. Fortunately the water was shallow, and they waded to shore. He added, "And we lost a good butcher knife."

He concludes thus, "God undertook in a marvelous way. We never needed much. As I look back now, I am thankful I had the chance to be there with the family. Those years at the camp are very pleasant memories for me, and I hope that those of you researching this movement will catch some of the enthusiasm and dedication which were such a rich part of those years."[1]

Elim Gospel Beach began as the dream of Rev. Valentine E. Nickel of Swift Current who is credited as the driving force in its acquisition. His dream was to have an interdenominational evangelistic and retreat center. (From page 1 of Elim Camp History by Grace Derksen Funk)

Let's Go Camping in the Arkansas Ozarks

"Its only twenty-five more miles," I said to my wife and three small children who were sitting in the backseat. We had traveled all day, and it was late afternoon. Our destination was Blanchard Springs where I would be participating in a camping program being sponsored by the mission at Culp, Arkansas. What I hadn't anticipated was that these twenty-five miles were Ozark miles. They were long miles, with lots of rocks and very crooked. There were numerous opportunities to make a wrong turn and we made our share of them. We would inquire for directions, but instructions were either vague, or we did not understand them. It was nearly dark when we arrived.

Blanchard Springs was an undeveloped public park, previously occupied by the Civilian Conservation Corps (CCC) and made available to Frank Horst, pastor of the Bethel Springs Mennonite Church at Culp, for a week of camping with his youth. We chose one of the six cabins and proceeded to make it "home sweet home." Everyone quickly adjusted to the primitive circumstances with no running water, except what we ran after down at the river. The flashlight was ample for getting everyone tucked in for the night. In those days campers were often expected to bring their own dishes and food, so getting a meal was no problem.

It didn't take too many ingredients to get a camping program together: the vision and enthusiasm of Frank Horst and his co-workers at the Culp mission and school; a few staff persons who could serve at no cost; some campers; and a place that would not cost anything. The campers were easy to find if the cost could be kept down to a couple of dollars. God provided a beautiful spot just twenty-five Ozark miles from Culp.

By noon the place was buzzing with activity. Youth, adults with small children, and boys and girls made up the community of campers who would be sharing life together for the next several days. Mountain folk are not difficult to get to know, and soon everyone was a big, happy family. There were the usual classes and activities for all of them. There was time to play and to enjoy social interaction. This was a first for all of them. What would church camp be like?

The river was shallow, but quite wide. It rippled past the camp over rocks and became quite warm from the sun's rays on the rocks. Like Ozark roads, it made lots of curves as it found its way through the valley. When the turns were abrupt, the water would wash a deeper place next to the bank. These provided swimming holes. We soon learned that early in the morning was the best time for taking your daily swim, because by midday the water in the river had warmed to a temperature that was not desirable for swimming. The river was used for many other things also. After each meal, campers went down to the river and washed their own dishes. Mothers went to the river with their babies when they needed attention, and when clothes needed to be laundered.

Much of the food was brought by families, and the rest had been brought by the staff from Culp. Meals were prepared and served in the open, for there was no kitchen. Classes were held outdoors. This is what some refer to as "real camping." The nights were peaceful and quiet except when the wild hogs would come into the camp. Sometimes the hogs got into a fight under the cabins, which were built on pilings above the ground.

The first camp at Blanchard Springs was held in 1945, and was continued for five years. The South Central Conference launched a mission program at about that time and the summer camping program was included. Each summer the program and facilities progressed from the circumstances of the first summer. Many people assisted in making these summer camps a meaningful experience for the people of the Culp community.[2]

Tillie (Yoder) Nauraine—Her Dream and Camp Ebenezer

"In spite of discipline difficulties, fatigue, weary minds, and emotional strain, no one on the staff would exchange their place with a king. In fact we were in business with the King of kings," wrote Tillie Yoder after a summer of camping with black children from the inner city with improvised facilities at her parents' farm near Millersburg, Ohio. The story begins in the early forties.

In her personal account of the Ebenezer story Tillie wrote: "A year ago when Laurence Horst spoke to the Christian Workers' Band at school I knew I must spend a summer in voluntary service work, even if it meant forfeiting a trip to the west coast with expenses paid and putting off nurses training. When I made application, two possibilities opened to me. One was at the Kansas City Children's Home and the other was to accompany an itinerary group to Alabama to work among blacks in Summer Bible School.

"I had almost decided on one of these, but there was that indelible imprint on my mind that I could not erase. I was haunted by the picture in my mind of ill-clad and undernourished black children in Chicago. Summer camping could bring them joy, and there they could receive instruction such as they had in Bible School. . . . Sin and vice run wild under the conditions in which they live. Some children are neglected and left to themselves. These we must help. After a great deal of deliberate planning, the program for Camp Ebenezer finally emerged.

"We had planned to care for fifteen children, but already there were twenty-two with staff. While this group was on their way back to Chicago, Brother James Lark called asking if we could ɘ twenty-five campers. We had twenty cots, twenty places at .e dining table. We were short on utensils to handle more than that. We told him we would do our best. When they arrived there were forty-one of them. We were floored. Every staff member felt this was a time to exercise their faith."

All of this was taking place at the farm home of the Jacob Yoders, Tillie's parents. There was an extra house in the back that had not been used for several years. It was put into service along with a large tent as the camp's facilities. In a case like this the staff lodged in the Yoder home, and the overflow of campers went to the living room of the Yoder home for sleeping. Campers had their own garden. When the older boys and girls were there one summer, they picked and canned sixty quarts of green beans, and sixty quarts of blackberries. They milked the cows, cleaned the chicken house, drove the tractor, and helped with other chores around the Yoder farm. The wheelbarrow was used for hauling water from the spring for laundry, showers, and other uses. It was also popular for just playing with when not in use otherwise. On rainy days they would go to the hayloft and slide down the rope to the barn floor. They would jump rope, and have wiener roasts on the hill.

The philosophy of the camp is found in this statement: "Summer camps bring to the deprived city child the blessings of life in the country and on the farm, and congenial group living in a Christian environment. Here for the first time the city child has the opportunity to run, romp and play with great hilarious freedom from the city with its fast-moving vehicles and crowds. Here for the first time many children see genuine Christian love in action. They see it in the lives of the staff with whom they work and play each day. Their experience must be more than a mere outdoor vacation. Every child at camp should come to some conscious understanding of the love of God in the practice of the Christian life."

The evangelistic emphasis was sincere but low key. They did not consider a group raising of the hand as evidence of accepting Christ as personal Savior. Campers would come to them in various ways and indicate their desire to be Christians. A 1950 brochure reports that nearly seventy-five boys and girls had made a decision for Christ through their camp experience. Twenty of these had been received into church fellowship in their home community. Bible instruction, devotions, evening chapel, and personal guidance were used in accomplishing their goals.

The camps did a great deal in building bridges between black and white. The children of the community would often join the black children at camp in play, and the campers would be entertained in the homes of the church members. The campers would see families come to camp with food and clothing for them. They were aware of the love that was being shared between them.

Camp Ebenezer operated five years and in three locations. The program did not die. Camp Luz owes much of its origin to Ebenezer. The spirit and philosophy of Camp Ebenezer and its founders keeps on living and is still reaching the lives of many. Children found God at Camp Ebenezer. They found him in the shady lane, in the meadow, in the hayloft, in the kitchen, in the dining room, and out in the fields behind a shock of wheat.[3]

The Camp Rehoboth Story

"There is room!" That was the statement of Rowena Lark when they located a suitable property for a summer camping program for black children outside of Chicago where she and her husband James were pastoring a church. The search had been long and frustrating. It seemed at times as if there was no place for them to establish a camping program to strengthen the Sunday school program of the Bethel Mennonite Church, and to give the boys and girls of their Sunday school a place to enjoy nature and experience Christian fellowship. When the Lord led them to Hopkins Park and to a ten-acre tract of land they could afford to purchase, it was only fitting to say, "Rehoboth! There is room!"

The Larks were a couple who were "on the move." They had vision and enthusiasm for using every possible means at their disposal to evangelize and nurture those around them. Christian camping was only one of the significant contributions this couple made. The ten-acre tract was soon put into use for the purpose for which it was intended. A space was quickly cleared and in a few days the camp was in progress. In 1952 the listing of Mennonite camps said of Camp Rehoboth: "A privately owned camp serving black children from the mission in Chicago. The buildings were set up with the help of Amos Bauman and a group of men from Goshen, Indiana. The program has been set up with the three-fold objective to help children worship, serve, and play in a Christian environment which they can not have at home."[4]

The Larks also saw the need for a Christian witness in the Hopkins Park community, and in 1949 monthly Sunday school services were begun. These grew into weekly services, along with an adult Bible class which was held in the post office building. Today the Rehoboth Mennonite Church has been organized to serve the residents of the area. Camping activities consist of day camping each summer. The last two days are spent on a camping trip, usually to a state park. They also sponsor canoe trips for their youth.

This provides another instance where the Sunday school and missionary emphasis of a pastor were instrumental in the outdoor ministry of Christian camping.

A Vision of a Different Sort

Dreams and concerns were surfacing in various ways and places during this period when an outdoor ministry was becoming reality in the churches. Those organizing and promoting Mennonite Youth Village represented the academic community and were advocating that the church become involved in a welfare program with children that would result in a chain of youth villages across the church, supervised and controlled by personnel that had been trained in the field of social services. Organized in 1949, they stated their purpose as follows:

> The purpose of the Mennonite Youth Village shall be to provide Christian homes for needy children; to promote the development of youth of a high physical, mental, moral, and spiritual character; and to instill in these youth the Anabaptist vision of faith and aggressive Christian love and outgoing service as the highest function of an active church. As much as possible, this shall be accomplished in a rural setting, through simple life with accent on the sanctity and importance of the Christian home as ordained of God.[5]

The program was carefully outlined and listed goals that would be used in implementing the objectives: (1) to establish a rural village of home units dedicated to the Christian nurture of children from broken homes; (2) to work closely and cooperatively with existing children's homes, and share welfare workers with them when possible; (3) to promote in the Mennonite Church an intensive publicity program leading to foster home care of needy children; (4) to promote the establishment of miniature villages or farm units in Mennonite communities throughout the United States, dedicated to the intensive care of children in need of homes; (5) to encourage and develop summer camps for children from underprivileged areas, and especially from cities; (6) to encourage the building of annexes to the homes in Mennonite communities with the view of establishing homes for broken families when the need arises; (7) to rehabilitate wherever possible those homes and parents capable of rehabilitation.

In a summary statement they said, "In all of the above activities the village would play a vital but fluid and flexible part; acting largely as a feeder and a center of rehabilitation; a dispenser of help and information; promoter of a healthy publicity program, and a center of child care in very needy areas."

Alta Schrock is credited with being the original instigator of the project, and was named its first executive director. The constitution that was drawn up and signed by the board in December of 1948 includes the names of Alta Schrock, Lester Glick, Paul Bender, Grant M. Stoltzfus, Howard C. Yoder, Robert Eckland, Ray E. Horst, and J. D. Graber. In its organization it became affiliated with the Board of Missions, and functioned through its Committee for Child Welfare.

Mennonite Youth Village was both a vision and a place. Early in its organization it acquired an eighty-acre farm near White Pigeon, Michigan, complete with farm buildings. The area is hilly and mostly forested. Camp buildings were placed on four different hill levels and spread out like a little campus. A welfare and mission emphasis was prominent in program throughout the years. Children attending were from low socioeconomic families, non-Mennonite background, and rural and city missions. Camps often integrated white, black, Indian, and Spanish children. The village had a capacity of sixty, and could accommodate as many as 400 children a season.

The history of Mennonite Youth Village was one of pioneering in various approaches to welfare camping. In the mid-seventies a new approach was used in which ten selected probationers of the Elkhart (Indiana) County Probation Department and the Cass (Michigan) County Department of Public Health were placed at Youth Village for a three-month period. In the city of Elkhart, Youth Village provided group homes for both boys and girls on a longer term basis. The philosophy of the program stressed preventive and corrective rather than punitive treatment for adolescents with problems.

In June, 1981, Youth Village closed due to lack of referrals and resulting financial losses. At that time the program included two group homes and a summer camp. The program sponsored by the Youth Village and the vision and inspiration of the early leaders in the movement provided a model and stimulus for others to follow as the ministry of Christian camping has established itself and has discovered so many different ways to be of service to the needs of society.

Other Unusual Beginnings of the 1940s

The story of the forties and its beginnings would not be complete without including two more stories. God was working in so many ways, and with different people in bringing about his plan for an outdoor ministry.

"Can the Winkler Bible Institute do something for the children of Winkler and the surrounding districts?" asked H. H. Redekop at a faculty meeting in the spring of 1949. The Winkler Bible Institute of the Mennonite Brethren in Manitoba had been active in their support of the Sunday School and Vacation Bible School movements. Now they were ready to reach out and expand these ministries with the establishment of a summer camp for children.

Instant response from the entire faculty and support and encouragement from the community put the idea into motion. H. H. Redekop and G. D. Pries were sent to locate a place suitable for the development of a camp. Their choice met with approval. Funds were solicited from friends, and $974 was received. By June of that same year, G. B. Dyck, C. I. Funk and others were clearing the place for the chapel. On July 10, 1949, the camp and its facilities were dedicated. The first director was George B. Dyck; the first workers were Salome Voth, June Hamm, Annie Janzen, Eva Dyck, John K. Wall, and Jake P. Wiebe. Their philosophy was apparent in that the first building was the chapel. Winkler Bible Camp stands as a memorial to the vision and dedication of this group of men and women who were the faculty of Winkler Bible Institute: the ones entrusted with the vision, and who followed their dreams.[6]

Camp Mennoscah near Murdock, Kansas, was brought into being by the interests and efforts of the Western District Youth Fellowship. The youth themselves assumed the financial responsibility for the purchase and development of a site that they could use to strengthen their existing retreat and camping programs. Their purchase was made in 1949, and their first activities were held that same year, using improvised facilities. It was not until 1962 that the Western District Conference assumed responsibility for its program and facilities.

Retreats for the young people of that area had started in 1925, with a retreat on the Bethel College campus, and later at Camp Wood near Elmdale, Kansas, and Camp Fellowship at Goddard, Kansas. The retreat movement was an established tradition, and had meant a lot to the youth. This prompted them to move ahead in something as daring as the establishment of Mennoscah. Their vision and efforts have been rewarded, and retreats and camping for all age groups were the result.

CHAPTER FIVE

The Fifties

A Decade of Building

The Fifties was the decade of
building and expansion of facilities:
for welfare camping and specialized programming;
of using camping as a tool for outreach
in missions and evangelism;
of sharing among camping people.

During the decade of the fifties the inter-Mennonite community of camps and retreats was destined to experience a record growth as compared to previous decades. During this time twenty-two permanent camps and retreat centers were established in the United States and Canada. The number of congregations and interest groups sponsoring programs with leased and improvised facilities was also on the increase. This was also the decade when camping staffs began to get together for sharing of ideas for program and development. The vision for expanding and strengthening the outdoor ministry of Christian camping was strong.

It was during this decade that a widespread interest was developed in welfare camping, specialized programming for underprivileged children or those with emotional or physical handicaps. Other groups were involved in missions and church planting and saw camping as a tool for outreach and evangelism. Minority and ethnic groups were included.

Of the twenty-two camps and retreat centers established in this decade by Mennonite conferences, thirteen of them were primarily concerned with welfare camping or as an outreach of mission work. The other nine were the result of existing church youth programs, and were designed for the youth of the church. Out of the twenty-one programs that were established during this same time using leased or improvised facilities, twelve of them conducted programs for children from city missions or for underprivileged or minority groups. The remaining nine were serving children and youth within the churches, and designed to strengthen the local program.

All of the Mennonite Brethren camps founded in this decade were related to mission and outreach. In the General Conference Mennonite Church two of the facilities were motivated by mission and outreach, and four of them were the result of existing youth programs in the church. The Mennonite Church established ten camp facilities whose primary purpose was a ministry to children and youth from city and rural missions, or for minority and emotionally disadvantaged youth and families. The other three were founded primarily for youth within the church.

Building facilities and developing program and philosophy were producing some unforeseen blessings. It was now possible to include groups and interests that were not included in the original plans, such as family camps and other special interest groups. Conferences, local congregations, and other organizations began to use the facilities to augment their programs of nurture and evangelism.

It was during this decade that program staffs began to include the teaching of outdoor skills, awareness of nature and of our relationship and responsibility to it, and respect for all of God's creation. Camp was becoming more than just a place for activity. The outdoor atmosphere and setting was becoming a tool for teaching. As a result, participants became known as "campers" rather than "retreaters." The term *retreat* was now coming to be used when a group met for some special interest, or for study and meditation, usually in an outdoor setting.

There was also a movement during this decade to bring camping staffs and personnel from various church agencies together for dialogue on common concerns. It had become apparent that the churches were now firmly involved in both an indoor and outdoor ministry. Even though there was a freedom for camping staffs to develop program and philosophy without specific guidance from the church, this freedom was exercised in a responsible way. At no time did the camping movement work at cross purposes with the church. Camping people often came to church agencies and boards in an effort to create meaningful relationships, and for the support that was needed from the larger church.

By the end of this decade camping was an established tradition in all of the Mennonite conferences. Successful experiences out of the earlier years affirmed the claims of its founders. S. F. Pannabecker, historian and churchman, wrote, "Church camps as one of the institutions of the church, represents the culmination of the retreat movement into a formal and calculated arm of the church reaching out to claim young people and introducing them into vital Christian living." He further commented that retreats and camps were doing in the General Conference Mennonite Church what the revival movement had accomplished in earlier times. A report to the triennial conference in 1951 stated, "Their effectiveness in winning converts and stimulating the Christian life has been amply demonstrated."[1]

The outstanding motive for the establishment of camps among the Mennonite Brethren in this decade was evangelism and outreach. When the Lawrence Warkentines went to Brandon, Manitoba, in 1956 to organize a group of believers into a church, they were aware of the value of summer camps for children. The following summer they leased facilities from the Eastern Missionary Society, and the Gospel Light Bible Camp was born. Redberry Bible Camp was founded by the Mennonite Brethren Home Missions in 1951. In the case of the Columbia Bible Camp in British Columbia, historian J. A. Toews says, "Here again the missionary character of the camp was evident from its inception.

In cooperation with the West Coast Children's Mission the society enrolled 168 children during the first summer. Over 40 decisions for Christ were recorded, most of them children from mission churches."[2]

In the Mennonite Church there was a tone of caution. How many camps are enough? During this decade, on the average, more than one new facility was established each year. In a report to the Mennonite Commission for Christian Education in 1956 this trend was addressed: "Camp directors feel they must have their own facilities. This is not necessarily correct. We need some good church camps, but they should be kept at a minimum. Improvised and leased facilities should be used where possible. We now have eight camps with six more under construction. If present trends continue, our program must grow or we will be overbuilt." But along with this note of caution there was a daring enthusiasm, and both facilities and programs grew. The conference of summer camp representatives that met in 1952 cautioned, "It is emphasized that the strong Christian life motivation behind all the camp programs should be continued, and that care should be taken to strengthen this central emphasis in all activities and to guard against falling into a purely recreational program."[3]

During this decade there were also many events that would affect camping and the youth of the churches. The United States had exploded its first hydrogen bomb. Both Russia and the United States had been successful in launching satellites. The United States' atom-powered submarine crossed under the polar icecap. One Soviet rocket orbited the sun; another circled the moon and sent back photographs. We had entered the space age. Campers would be coming from a different world in the future.

During this rapid change of events and lifestyles it was not uncommon for staff and campers to have difficulty understanding each other. Many camp directors discovered that college sophomore counselors and junior high campers had difficulty in communicating. It was common for staff to be answering the questions they had about life, rather than recognizing the real needs of the camper.

Significant Beginnings in the 1950s

1950 - **Tel-Hai Camp**, Pennsylvania, established by an association of interested persons within the *Mennonite Church* to provide facilities for inner-city children.

Hopi Indian Youth Camp, Arizona, sponsored by *Hopi Indian Mennonite churches (GC)* to provide a camp apart

from the intertribal camps, using leased facilities, continued for several years.

Camp Friedenswald, Michigan, established by the Central District of the *General Conference Mennonite
Church* to provide facilities for a growing youth program.

Stringer Ranch Camp, Colorado, operated in improvised facilities and sponsored by *Colorado Mennonite
churches (MC)* prior to Rocky Mountain Camp.

Youth retreats, Arizona, sponsored by the *Arizona
Mennonite churches (MC)* and the Saguaro Club, a youth
organization starting in 1946.

1951 - **Tent Meeting**, Virginia, sponsored by the *Mennonite
churches of Virginia and West Virginia (MC)*, held in a
tent on the Robert See farm and credited as the beginning
of events that resulted in Highland Retreat.

Camps for children, Pennsylvania, sponsored by the
Franconia Conference of Mennonites (MC), for children
from city missions, using the facilities of Camp Men-O-
Lan.

Redberry Bible Camp, Saskatchewan, established by
the Northern District of the *Mennonite Brethren* as an
outreach for the mission program of the churches.

1952 - **Northern Michigan Youth Camp**, Michigan, organized
and sponsored by twelve *Mennonite churches of
northern Michigan (MC)*, using leased facilities.

Rocky Mountain Mennonite Camp, Colorado, established by interested persons within the *Mennonite
Church* to provide facilities for the growing program of
camping in Colorado and surrounding states.

Eden Bible Camp, Ontario, established by the *Mennonite Brethren church of Ontario*. The Youth Committee
recommended building an auditorium at Eden School to
provide facilities for a youth camp.

Camp Emmaus, Illinois, leased facilities used by the *Illinois Mennonite churches (MC)* for their camps prior to
Menno Haven.

1953 - **Youth camping program**, Ontario, sponsored by the
Mennonite Brethren, using leased facilities.

Camp Luz, Ohio, established by an association of interested persons within the *Mennonite Church* to provide
facilities for the Camp Ebenezer and their existing youth
retreats.

Bible Memory Camps, Indiana, sponsored by the *Bible
Memory Program, Inc.* Bible memorization required for
camp attendance. Summer camping program uses leased

facilities in several states. Headquarters at Goshen, Indiana.

1954 - **Swan Lake Christian Camp**, South Dakota, established by the Northern District of the *General Conference Mennonite Church.*

Camp Moose Lake, Manitoba, established by *Conference of Mennonites of Manitoba (GC).* Developed by the Manitoba Conference and the Moose Lake Fellowship.

Black Rock Retreat, Pennsylvania, established by Frank Enck for inner-city children. An association of interested persons within the *Mennonite Church* was organized for development of the camp and its operation.

1955 - **Children's camps** introduced in British Columbia by the *General Conference Mennonite Church.* Prior to the founding of Camp Squeah, leased facilities were used.

Young people's retreats introduced by the *Mennonite churches (MC) of North Dakota.*

Children's camps introduced in Florida for migrant and inner-city children; sponsored by *Eastern Mennonite Mission Board (MC)*, using leased facilities.

Children and youth camps, Missouri, sponsored by *Lakeside Mennonite Camp Association.* Camping activities had preceded the organization of this association. Leased and improvised facilities were used.

Fraser Lake Camp, Ontario, established by an association of interested persons in the *Mennonite Church* in the interest of city children.

1956 - **Alder Creek Camp**, Oregon, established as the site for the continuation of the Oregon youth camping program, sponsored by the *Mennonite Church.*

Youth retreats introduced by the *Idaho Mennonite churches (MC).* Definite date of beginning not documented.

Youth camping program introduced by the New Breman *Mennonite Church in New York.*

Specialized programming for delinquent youth introduced by *Rocky Mountain Mennonite Camp*, Colorado, which resulted in the year-round programs at Frontier Boys Camp and Brockhurst Boys Ranch in Colorado.

Gospel Light Bible Camp, Ontario, sponsored by the *Mennonite Brethren churches of Manitoba*, using the facilities of Covenant Bible Church.

Camp Shalom, Ontario, established and operated by the *Mennonite Ontario Hebrew Mission* for Jewish families;

MENNONITE CAMPING PROGRAMS BEGUN IN THE 1950s

This map shows the approximate location of the 44
camping and retreat programs begun in the 1950s.
Beginning dates and names are shown in the
chronological listing for the 1950s.

■ Permanent facilities
O Improvised or leased facilities

in operation for several years.

Young peoples retreats introduced in the *Mennonite churches of Nebraska (MC)*.

Pike Lake Bible Camp, Saskatchewan, established by the *Conference of Mennonites of Saskatchewan (GC)*. Discontinued in 1977 and the property sold. It is now replaced with the newly developed Shekinah Retreat Centre.

Camp Hebron, Pennsylvania, established by an association of interested persons within the *Mennonite Church*.

Youth retreat sponsored by the *Iowa City Mennonite Church* at Delhi State Park.

1957 - **Bethel Mennonite Camp**, Kentucky, established and operated by the *Conservative Mennonite Mission Board*, Irwin, Ohio.

Palisades Mennonite Camp, Idaho, developed by the Palisades *General Conference Mennonite Church*. Facilities are on a government lease in the mountains.

South Texas Youth Camping, sponsored by the *Mennonite churches* of the area and the *South Central Mennonite Conference (MC)* for Latin-American youth, using leased facilities. Discontinued after several years.

Camp Amigo, Michigan, established by an association of interested persons within the *Mennonite Church*. Founded to provide facilities for Bible Memory Program and growing retreat movement.

1958 - **Mountain Youth for Christ**, West Virginia, sponsored by the *mountain congregations of West Virginia*, using leased facilities.

Columbia Bible Camp, British Columbia, established by the *British Columbia Mennonite Brethren churches* and the *Columbia Bible Camp Society* in the interest of missions and outreach.

Woodcrest Retreat, Pennsylvania, developed by an association of interested persons within the *Mennonite Church* to provide camping for recreational vehicles and summer day camping.

Camp Menno Haven, Illinois, established by an association of interested persons within the *Mennonite Church*.

Highland Retreat of the Mennonite Church, Virginia, established by an association of interested persons within the *Mennonite Church*; it was conceived as a Bible conference grounds for the smaller congregations in the mountains of Virginia and West Virginia.

Hidden Acres Mennonite Camp and Retreat Centre,

Ontario, established by an association of interested persons within the *Mennonite Church* to provide facilities for children's camps.

Ootsa Lake Bible Camp, British Columbia, sponsored and maintained by a committee from the *General Conference Mennonites* of the Abbotsford and Burns Lake areas.

God at Work—Passing Out Dreams and Visions

On a crisp winter evening in January 1950, a group of men gathered in the living room of Simon Zook at Honey Brook, Pennsylvania. The question for discussion was: Does this group want to buy a farm? The reason: to provide a camp for children from the city. When the time came to vote by secret ballot, the answer was a unanimous yes. Abner Zook, who was active in a witness to Jewish people in New York City, had visited Camp Ebenezer in Ohio, which had been established for black children from the city. He felt this kind of ministry would be an effective way to reach the children of New York City. He emphasized that the program should be missionary and evangelistic in nature. Clarence Fretz of the Philadelphia Mennonite Mission also expressed his interest in establishing such a camp.

The vision soon expanded to something more than just a place for disadvantaged children. They began to talk about young people's activities, Bible conferences, and family activities. They even shared their vision with each other that perhaps it could include a home for the aged. By 1951 *Camp Tel Hai* near Honey Brook, Pennsylvania, was in operation with 150 children mostly from New York City attending over the summer. The project now includes all that had been dreamed of that evening in January, 1950.[4]

* * * * * * * * * * * * * * * * * * *

J. N. Hoeppner, Rev. Paul J. Schaefer, and Rev. P. A. Rempel were all on the same committee, the Manitoba Mennonite Youth Organization of the Conference of Mennonites of Manitoba. The committee shared many concerns regarding youth work, and often they would get around to sharing their visions about a camp for youth. They wanted to share this concern with others, but when their dream reached the conference floor, the word *camp* had negative implications to many. There would be a beach, and good things didn't happen at a beach. The idea did not get approval, but these men did not quit. Their dream did not just go away. These men were well known and respected, and people listened.

For Sale: Sunnyside Beach on the Assiniboine River, $15,000. This was all it took to put the wheels in motion. The beach had been a place for dances, drinking, and other non-Christian activities. But Rev. William H. Enns said to himself, his church, and others, "This is our God-given opportunity. The conference should buy it, and change it into a place for Christian activities."

The conference was not ready, but an interest group was organized and the beach was purchased. Camp Assiniboine was prepared by volunteers, mostly from the Springstein congregation, but also from the south. The program was set up by Rev. Paul J. Schaefer, Rev. P. A. Rempel, J. N. Hoeppner, and A. A. Teichroew. H. H. Goertzen and J. A. Wiebe also had a part in the preparing of the first camp.

The large auditorium served as kitchen and girl's dorm. Several small cabins with leaky roofs housed the boys. Kitchen utensils were very limited and table service was scarce. There was one piece for each camper—either a fork, a knife, or a spoon. Bowls for breakfast cereal did not go around, so some campers ate cereal from a saucer.

Children attending camp were nine to fifteen years of age, and were expected to have learned 150 Bible verses. The aim of the camp was to bring children into a personal relationship with Christ through singing, Bible stories, and devotions. Recreational equipment was limited, and the river that provided swimming was not safe for small children.

In 1957 *Moose Lake Camp* was started to care for the overflow of Camp Assiniboia, and was originally syncronized with the Assiniboine program. In 1963 *Camp Koinonia* was established to complete the family of camps for the Conference of Mennonites in Manitoba, known as Camps with Meaning. God continued to raise up men and women with vision as the ministry of outdoor camping included more people, young and old, each succeeding year.[5]

* * * * * * * * * * * * * * * * * * * *

"Prudence and I loaded our belongings into our '36 Ford pulling our newly donated twenty-foot house trailer to Pinecraft, Sarasota, Florida." This is the way Harvey Birky would often begin his story when telling how he and his wife answered the call of God when they received the vision to work with children in a *Bible Memory* camping ministry. He continues, "We went by faith, not knowing exactly what God had in mind, or just how the program would develop."

After spending a year in Florida, the Lord led them to the Children's Bible Mission, Birmingham, Alabama. Here, they along with others were contacting over 10,000 children a month in the public schools.

In 1953 the program took them to begin a work in the Indiana-Michigan area with eighteen campers. By 1958 this had grown to include nearly 200 campers. Children enrolled in the Bible Memory program were eligible to attend the camps which were begun in Missouri, Ohio, Illinois, Iowa, Oregon, Arkansas, and Oklahoma, with campers enrolling from neighboring states. In 1980 there were 600 enrolled in the seven weeks of Bible Memory camp in five different states.[6]

* * * * * * * * * * * * * * * * * * *

The vision for an outdoor ministry for Jewish families was given to J. Ross and Shirley Goodall, who were directors of *Camp Shalom*, sponsored by the Ontario Hebrew Mission. Founded in 1956 near Kearney, Ontario, its purpose and program was to provide a place and ministry for Jewish families where they could find fellowship in a Christian atmosphere away from their everyday world in the city. It was located on 100 acres on a private lake. Its facilities included a lodge and several smaller buildings. The program was loosely structured, and included the entire family. Families could come and go at their own convenience during the camping season. Most families attending were non-Christian. The camp and its program continued for a number of years.[7]

* * * * * * * * * * * * * * * * * * *

The Welfare Board of the Ontario Mennonite Conference began sharing their concerns and vision for a camping ministry for underprivileged city children as early as 1950. The vision did not go away, even though lack of interest on the part of some and other obstacles kept it from developing into its first camp in 1955. In an effort to make the program a reality, J. C. Fretz suggested the idea of city children coming to the farm homes of Christian people for a week or so. This did not seem feasible and did not work out. Then Oscar Snyder offered his farm, the mission board voted $300 for up-front money, three tents were purchased, and other miscellaneous equipment was rounded up. Children attended camp at this improvised farm setting for five years.

* * * * * * * * * * * * * * * * * * *

Campo de Amistad, along Lake Mathis in Texas, 1959, was the vision of a group of young people serving in a voluntary service unit under the sponsorship of the Mennonite Board of Missions. Their ministry was among the Hispanic population of southern

Texas where a number of Mennonite fellowships had been established.

This program was an annual event beginning in the early fifties. One of their reports read, "Approximately fifteen boys made commitments, seven of which were from the same cabin. Because of the wide age range the boys were divided into two age groups for many of their activities. The entire program was an inspiration to all who attended."

In one of the girls' camps a counselor reported, "Some of the girls in my cabin had never had their own devotions before. They had never prayed to God in their own words. The first morning we sat on the grass under a tree during our devotions and discussed what it means to pray. The second morning I sent each one alone to read several verses, and then talk to God just as you would to your friend. A few minutes later we met to discuss what we had found in our Bible passages. They returned with shining faces. 'We prayed!' they exclaimed. This union with God had given them a real joy and closeness with God as their Creator."

* * * * * * * * * * * * * * * * * * * *

Mt. Eldon Christian Conference Center is surrounded by the city of Flagstaff, Arizona, although it wasn't planned that way. As early as 1894 the General Conference of Mennonites established Christian mission work among the Hopi Indians. Other denominations followed. They formed a fellowship with a vision for Christian camps and conferences as a very important part of their mission to the Indians of the Southwest.

In 1914 this fellowship of Indians and white Christians purchased thirty-eight acres five miles out of Flagstaff at the foot of Mt. Eldon. This camping movement soon grew into large gatherings. Friends of the Christian Indians were also invited, and many found the Lord there. Others dedicated their lives for Christian service. Among these was a young man by the name of Theodore Epp, son of the Rev. J. B. Epp, Mennonite missionary to the Hopis.

In 1949 the Hopi Mennonite churches started a week of camp for their youth, but later in order to get the Hopi youth into the larger fellowship of Christians from all tribes, they included their youth in the larger gatherings. In more recent years the tribes of the Southwest have developed strong leadership in their own tribes, and have begun family camps among their own people. These camps are planned by their leaders and to a large degree are carried on in their own language and using their ways of feeding and housing their people. Indians from all over America attend these gatherings now held on what was the thirty-five acres five miles east of Flagstaff, but now surrounded by city. The vision and spirit of these early Mennonite missionaries, like the grain of mustard seed, has grown and is blessing the lives of thousands of people, as the kingdom of God is expanded through this ministry.[8]

* * * * * * * * * * * * * * * * * * *

Black Rock Retreat, the first Mennonite camp of Lancaster County and of the Lancaster Conference had its beginning in 1954. The man endowed with the vision was Frank Enck. His vision was a camp for city children, the unchurched, the disadvantaged. He saw camping as an arm of the church.

Enck waited and watched for a piece of property in Lancaster County that would be suitable, and when God led him to this place, he purchased it. His plans were to move ahead step by step, but when others heard of his venture of faith they urged him to go ahead at once and pledged their support. Frank chose the name from the black rock spring, symbolic of the never-failing source of supply.

Not everyone agreed with, or understood the vision God had given to Frank. "Don't you know those grounds are infested by snakes?" "Will people want to camp here with only one way to get out in case of fire? What will you do?" When men and women with vision and dreams are obedient to God, things are bound to happen.

The first camp was held in 1957 with seventeen girls, black and white, from the South Christian Street Mission. They slept on cots and in sleeping bags on the auditorium floor. The first Sunday evening service was held in June 1956 with 300 present.

Frank was not privileged to live and see his dreams develop into the ministry it has grown to be, but the camp continues to honor the vision of its founder. Eighty-five percent of its campers come from the inner city, the unchurched, the disadvantaged. Thirteen different youth agencies were referring campers to them in the early 1980s. Two weeks are reserved for the mentally handicapped referred by the Lancaster Association for Retarded Citizens, an annual event for the past fifteen years.

* * * * * * * * * * * * * * * * * * *

Fraser Lake Camp and the Emerson McDowell Story

Emerson McDowell (1918-1976) stands out as a pioneer in the outdoor ministry of Christian camping. His vision took him beyond the thinking of many for the potential for camping. Sensitive to the needs of boys and girls, he saw the outdoors and nature as a place and tool for teaching them about God and creation. His vision called for action, and he started in very simple ways. The story is best told by Elsie McDowell as she wrote it for the twenty-fifth anniversary of Fraser Lake Camp in 1979:

In the early summer of 1955 Emerson McDowell made a long-distance call from Toronto to Elvon Burkholder at Fort Stewart, Ontario. The connection was poor, the conversation not too satisfactory, and when it was over, he hoped Elvon had understood him correctly. The ministers from the three Toronto Mennonite churches were planning to bring some children to the Burkholder farm at Fort Stewart for a week of outdoor living. There must have been some previous communication, but from this point on, plans were set in motion. Announcements were printed and distributed in the community along with the Summer Bible School invitation. This would be a Christian camp under the pastor's supervision.

On August 1 a colorful caravan left Toronto for Fort Stewart for one week of boys camp. Al Smith drove a van, several men drove cars filled with eager boys, and one car hauled a trailer loaded with luggage and the "Glenhill Cruiser," the homemade canoe. . . . Three tents were set up in the front yard for sleeping. In a large summer kitchen at the back of the farmhouse there was enough space for cooking and eating. Long plank tables were arranged and 40 people could be seated at one time. Activities included climbing trees, watching the farmer milk his cows, and playing with the kittens. It was a half hour walk for swimming and boating. . . .

Girls were taken to camp the following week. A threatening storm the next to last day caused the girls to leave their tents and carry their sleeping bags into the Burkholder's house. Their shoes were left on the porch and they were admonished to be very quiet because there was a new baby in the house. Upstairs, in two rooms, 30 girls and their counselors lay in neat rows like sardines in a can. . . . According to the records 23 boys with a staff of 5, and 30 girls with a staff of 6, had enjoyed a farm holiday at the Burkholder farm.[9]

Fraser Lake Camp was destined to become reality, to become a place and a legend, in the hearts of hundreds of boys and girls under the leadership and inspiration of Emerson and his colleagues.

Camping with Juvenile Delinquents at Rocky Mountain Camp

The mountain air was crisp and clear on that Saturday morning of August 1956. Coming up the winding mountain road leading from the highway to Rocky Mountain Mennonite Camp was a caravan of cars, loaded with campers. These were not the usual run of campers. All of them were under the jurisdiction of the Denver Juvenile Court and were being brought to camp by their probation officers. Society had labeled them *juvenile delinquents*.

At the camp awaiting their arrival was a staff who had committed themselves to providing a meaningful camping experience to these youth who were in trouble. "If camping is good for our church boys and girls, it will also be a good experience for kids like this." That is what they had been saying to each other, but this theory would soon be tested. Specific plans had not been formulated. In general, the program would consist of simple living in this outdoor setting, and relating to the campers in a positive way.

The cars pulled up in front of the lodge. Heads were sticking out the opened windows. There were expressions and feelings of anxiety, fear, wonderment. Now what? Suddenly the car doors all opened at once, and campers piled out. Thirty-one boys and four girls. Staff and campers sized each other up, and the staff attempted to welcome the youth to camp.

Every possible emotion was in play at some point around camp for the next several hours—suspicion, hatred, love, anger, distrust, and fear. In the lodge campers and staff faced each other, along with the probation officers, and went over some basic ground rules. Rules being given by strangers did not do much to relieve the tension and suspicion that already existed. The physical surroundings were in direct contrast to the city from which the campers had just come. By noon campers and counselors were settled in their tents and the officers were on their way back to Denver. Before leaving they assured the staff that if trouble developed, they should get in touch, and they would come after the campers and return them to Denver. Some of the statements the officers made, and some of their body language suggested to the staff that they would probably be returning in a couple of days.

The staff was made up of persons who had accepted the teachings of Jesus in the Sermon on the Mount as being a statement of the way the Christian life is to be lived. In these new circumstances they just acted natural, with no pretense or show. This only added to the confusion and frustration. The campers felt that the kindness of the staff toward them was a snow job. Accepting this love was a risk. They assumed the staff was setting a trap for them, or would be asking favors.

It was not until the middle of the week that a semblance of

communication began to surface. In the meantime there had been no violence, and while camp life was often turbulent, things never got out of hand. The norms the campers had established for life worked pretty well for them in the city, but in this simple setting it was different. In Denver the larger society could absorb them, and their delinquency was not as apparent to them and to each other as it was here. All at once their world had shrunk to only a few people, and living had been reduced to simple dimensions. In Denver they were the tough kids. They still were, and the staff did not argue the point with them, but it soon became apparent to the staff that they were above all possessed with fear. They were living in prisons they had built around themselves. They feared life itself. Their dominant question was how they could best escape the realities of life.

In the maintenance area was a small gasoline engine on a cement mixer. A few of the boys appeared to be taking special interest in this engine. Maybe they were mechanically minded. Soon the staff got smart. They saw that by cupping their hands over a container of gasoline and inhaling deeply several times the boys would experience a high for about a half hour. Some campers tried other things too. Three of them took some turpentine from the craft shop and some diesel fuel from a storage building, mixed the two together, and went up the mountain back of the camp where two of them drank it. The third boy came running back to camp with the news that his buddies up on the mountain were dying. They were laid on their cots in their tent while staff tried to find out what they had taken so the proper remedies could be prescribed. A law of the gang was that no one ever "ratted off." In no way was one going to tell on the other. Finally between cries of pain, one of them said, "We might as well tell them. We're going to die anyway." A trip to the emergency room and a stomach pump took care of the situation. When asked why they did it, they replied, "Just for kicks."

During the week there were many positive and happy experiences. There were long hikes in the high mountain country of Colorado, often above timberline at over 12,000 feet. The crafts program was challenging to some of them. There were some meals cooked out in the open. They sometimes slept under the stars. They were experiencing love and caring from the staff. No one was swearing at them. They were not being threatened with physical violence. No one was becoming angry with them, even when they could have. Out on the playing field they were discovering the fun of being part of a team. The staff and campers sat around the campfire and told stories and sang together. They were being exposed to values and a way of life that had been foreign to them.

The following Saturday morning was a beautiful day just like the one a week before when the campers arrived. All preparations had been made for their return to Denver. Bags were packed, and ready to load. But there was a freedom among the campers much different from when they arrived. They were out on the playing field, or at other places that had become dear to them. A caravan of cars wound its way up the mountain road to the camp coming for the campers. There were anxious inquiries from the officers. How have things gone? One of them said, "If we had found the staff sitting around with cigarettes hanging out of their mouths and shooting a game of crap, then we would know who came out on top." To their surprise they discovered the campers were not that anxious about returning to Denver.

When the staff found themselves alone again they drew a deep breath and started to sort out their emotions and to evaluate the week and its experiences. Had anything been accomplished? Was anyone helped? Did they even have a good time? Would the staff ever know?

Back in Denver the campers returned to their normal routine of life. Each had to report to his or her probation officer and to the staff psychologist. One of the boys had made a complete turn-around and had found a new sense of values and direction for life. But Dr. Parimba, the staff psychologist, discovered that something unusual had happened to each of the campers. All of them were expressing some positive attitudes about themselves and about life. He called this to the attention of Phillip Gilliam, judge of the Denver Juvenile Court. Dr. Parimba's curiosity was at work. How could this happen in one week to so many?

When the same program was repeated the following summer, Dr. Parimba came to camp to observe. He watched. He listened. He talked to the campers and then to staff. He asked staff what they were doing, and how? All they could say was that they were providing an atmosphere of love and security. To satisfy himself he came up with the premise that in this atmosphere the staff was mixing up the camper's cues, and this required them to establish a new set of norms. This was not what the staff was trying to do. They were just accepting the campers as people of worth and relating to them in Christian love. This interaction was being used by God to change attidues from negative to positive.

This program continued for several years at Rocky Mountain Camp. It was expanded each summer to include more boys and girls, and for longer periods of time. In telling about the camp's program at a meeting of a civic group in Denver, Judge Gilliam told how the program had kept 300 boys out of his court during the year. He went on to explain that he was sending the leaders to the camp, and this prevented them from getting others involved. He told Jess Kauffman, the director, "When I first met you I thought you were another do-gooder, and that your organization was like many others. But I thought, 'I have given other do-gooders a chance, only to see them fail. Why not give your group a chance too?' " Then he added, "You should know that I put you to the test that first summer. I rounded up the meanest bunch of kids I could find in Denver. They were the leaders and the trouble-makers." God was honoring the efforts of ordinary Christian people who were being obedient to a vision God had given them. In 1960, by unanimous vote of the staff of the Denver Juvenile Court, their plaque of the year was awarded to the camp and its program for outstanding service to the youth of Denver.

This specialized programming led to the development of a year-round rehabilitation program for boys. After success with the Denver court, other agencies also referred campers.[10]

CHAPTER SIX

The Sixties

*A Decade of Expansion,
of New Development,
of Program Changes*

The Sixties was a decade of contradiction,
confusion and conflict in society.
Youth were distressed with inconsistencies they saw.
Basic trust had deteriorated.
The outdoor ministry of Christian camping was especially needed
at this time, giving youth freedom
to dialogue, to search, to develop positive attitudes.

Camping in the Mennonite and Brethren in Christ conferences experienced a steady growth in the sixties, both in acceptance and in the development of new facilities and programs. Twenty-four new campsites and retreat centers were established in the United States and Canada. Numerous other programs were sponsored by local congregations using improvised or leased facilities. These not only provided outdoor experiences for children and youth, but also included families and interest groups.

In the camping community much of the emphasis in this decade was on mission outreach, both to children of the community and to children from local congregations and missions. As many as half of the youth and children attending Mennonite camps were from either non-Mennonite or unchurched homes. This pattern provided a friendship evangelism that was instrumental in bringing many youth into the fellowship of the church. It also made possible a witness to those who would not attend the churches. In this way the ministry of local congregations was increased and strengthened.

During the decade two programs were established on a year-round basis for the rehabilitation of delinquent youth—Frontier Forest Camp in Ontario and Frontier Boys Camp in Colorado. Both programs were successful and operated for a number of years. The Mennonite Board of Missions sponsored the biking program known as Out-Spokin' which provided bicycle trips in the United States, Canada, and overseas. There continued to be an interest in welfare camping, and five camps were established with this as the primary goal. Existing camps also held special weeks for those with emotional and physical handicaps.

For society at large the sixties have been recorded as the decade of tumult and change—a time of repeated tragedy and assassinations. It was also the decade when man first walked on the moon. Youth were distressed with the inconsistencies they saw around them. Demonstrations and revolts were common. There were violent attacks upon the establishment and its traditions. The Vietnam War ground on. Many youth made deep commitments, even dangerous commitments, toward making the world what they thought it could be

It was a decade of contradication, confusion, and conflict. Two struggles stand out: the young struggling to change the bureaucracy-bound establishment, and the blacks in their struggle to possess their long overdue rights.

The outdoor ministry of the church was especially valuable in these times. The youth within the churches were being affected and were involved in the spirit of the times. They were being told that God had died. It was a time when many youth were rejecting

Christianity or going underground with their faith. In the informal atmosphere of camps and retreats they could talk, share, ask questions, and get answers and opinions. Questions and comments that would not have been accepted in the Sunday school or traditional church setting could surface in this atmosphere where searching and finding was more probable. Its genius was in developing attitudes that made growth possible.

Those involved in leadership during this time were well aware that these changes and influences in society were affecting the direction of camping. A rapidly changing world was leaving a gap between age groups, and young adults were having difficulty relating to younger campers. Camping techniques were experiencing change, and staffs were being forced to experiment and search for new methods. Many of the earlier camping and retreat programs were patterned after the Bible conference. During this decade some camping programs experienced the other extreme of decentralized programming where cabin leaders and campers planned their own day within the framework established for them. It contained little, if any structure. From one extreme to another, program staffs arrived at a program technique that provided for structure when needed, yet with a freedom that encouraged creative planning.

Typical of the urgency expressed in the sixties is this statement taken from a report to the Mennonite Commission for Christian Education in 1966:

> The urgency on the camping question as I see it is this: The Mennonite Camping Association is aware that they have on their hands a movement that is about to break loose across the church as a tidal wave. They are fully aware that Christian camping has a potential for immeasurable good in the church as other movements have in the past. But it needs guidance. It needs to be seen as a part of what the total Mennonite Church will be tomorrow. It must not be a side show, or an escape from the congregation, or in any way become competitive. We have not yet spelled out what a viable educational philosophy of church camping would look like in the light of our educational objectives. The Mennonite Camping Association is asking us for help on this question. Camps are already here. It would be most unfortunate if we would force camping to make its own way, to develop its own model, then later come into the church through the back door as did the Sunday school in the past.[1]

Before the close of the decade a statement of philosophy had been written and given general approval. During this time special attention was being given to the development of philosophy and curriculum. Camping staffs were trying to find a common ground on what the movement was to accomplish, and to establish a rationale for its existence. Conferences and seminars provided opportunity for camping people to share in their efforts to maximize their opportunities that were being entrusted to them in Christian camping.

The camping movement was confronted with factors characteristic of the decade. These were realities that could not be ignored. Basic trust had deteriorated. The moral fiber of society had hit a new low. Society was faced with the possibility of becoming two societies unless it would open up to the disadvantaged. There was an increase of leisure time with the introduction of automation and a new work ethic which was demanding shorter hours and higher wages. An affluent society had established its own value systems and priorities. All of these were affecting the Christian camping program and its technique of programming.

There was still caution being expressed about the number of camps being established. Were we overdoing a good thing? In 1966 Edith Herr, secretary of Church Camps for the Mennonite Commission for Christian Education cautioned: "Are we building too many camps? Are we developing beyond our needs?" In the decade in which she was reporting, the Mennonite Church alone had developed twelve new facilities. The Commission replied, "It is not how many camps we have that is important. What is happening because of them is our concern." Earlier in the decade it was suggested by some of the church leaders that possibly the church at large should be alerted to the danger of "moving too fast." Yet, in that same year reporting indicated that only 10 percent of the children attending the Mennonite Sunday schools were going to camp.

Many camps that had been developed previously were expanding and winterizing. In the earlier development it was usually anticipated that the camps would be used only during the summer months. Now winter programming was becoming popular, especially where snowfall permitted winter snow sports. Cross country skiing was introduced. Toboggan runs were constructed. Interest groups were waiting for an opportunity to use the camp's facilities, and by making them available during all four seasons many more groups could be accommodated. The outdoor ministry of Christian camping had progressed to another plateau of growth and acceptance, although it was destined to experience more growth in these areas in the coming decade.

Significant Beginnings in the 1960s

1960 - **Camp Loma De Vida**, Texas, established in the Latin-
American community of south Texas by the *Mennonite
Brethren* and other evangelical Christians. In its beginning it was supported primarily by MB. Now owned and
operated as interdenominational, MB had camping activities in this area prior to Loma De Vida.

Silver Lake Mennonite Camp, Ontario, established by
the Ontario Youth Organization of the *General Conference Mennonite Church*. Now sponsored by the United
Mennonite Churches of Ontario.

Frontier Boys Camp, Colorado, a year-round rehabilitation program for delinquent youth. A spin-off of the specialized camps at *Rocky Mountain Mennonite Camp*.
Sponsored by the Barnabas Club, a group of interested
parties from interdenominational backgrounds.

Frontier Forest Camp, Ontario, a program for juvenile
delinquents operated the first year at *Fraser Lake Mennonite Camp*. Property for developing Frontier Forest Camp
was purchased and facilities added. The program operated until 1970.

Drift Creek Camp, Oregon, established by an association of interested persons within the *Mennonite Church*.
Facilities developed on leased government property.

1961 - **Spruce Lake Retreat**, Pennsylvania, established by an
association of interested persons within the *Mennonite
Church*. They operate a two-prong program at two sites; a
wilderness setting for youth and a conference and retreat
center.

Spruce Lake Wilderness Camp, Pennsylvania, an extension of *Spruce Lake Retreat*. Their program for youth
dates back to 1951, using leased facilities.

Camp Squeah, British Columbia, established and operated by the *Conference of Mennonites of British Columbia
(GC)*.

Camp Valaqua, Alberta, established and operated by the
Conference of Mennonites of Alberta (GC). As early as
1955 the Alberta Mennonite Youth Organization sponsored camping activities, using leased facilities.

Camps for youth, Virginia and West Virginia, sponsored
by the *Mennonite churches (MC)* of the area.

Youth camps, Alabama and Northwest Florida District of
the *Lancaster Mennonite Conference (MC)*, using leased
facilities.

1962 - **Jubilee Bible Camp**, Manitoba, sponsored by the *Mennonite Brethren* Newton Community Fellowship Church, and the Portage Evangelical Mennonite Church. Mennonite Brethren started using the camp in 1962 for youth groups and families.
Deer Creek Christian Camp, Colorado, established by an association of interested persons within the *Mennonite Brethren Church*. Now interdenominational in operation.
Hidden Acres Mennonite Camp and Retreat Centre, Ontario, established by an association of interested persons within the *Mennonite Church* with emphasis on children with emotional and physical handicaps, as well as programs for all age groups within the church.
Camp Freedom, Florida, developed and operated by the *Brethren in Christ*. Program consists of Bible camps for children and youth, and retreats and conferences for adults and families.
Camp Kahquah, Ontario, developed and operated by the *Brethren in Christ*. Program consists of Bible camps for children and youth, and retreats and conferences for adults and families.
1963 - **Camp Koinonia**, Manitoba, established and operated by the *Conference of Mennonites in Manitoba (GC)*.
1964 - **Camp Evergreen**, Alberta, established and operated by the *Conference of Mennonites of Alberta (GC)*. Camps for youth had been held at leased facilities for several years prior to founding the camp.
Camp Lakeview, Michigan, jointly owned by the Central District of the *Brethren in Christ* and the Michigan District of the Missionary Church. Operate year around for children, youth, adults, and rental groups.
1965 - **Bethany Birches Camp**, Vermont, established by an association of interested persons within the *Mennonite Church*. Church planting resulted in three Mennonite churches in Vermont in 1949. The camp supplements their outreach to the community.
Mile High Pines Camp, California, established by the Pacific Conference of *Brethren in Christ* and the California District of the Wesleyan Church. Operated year-round for all ages.
Miracle Camp, Michigan, established and operated by the *Evangelical Mennonite Brethren*. This is their only camp, but they are active in a camping ministry with other evangelicals.
1966 - **Camping for youth**, Ontario, introduced by the *Menno-*

MENNONITE CAMPING PROGRAMS BEGUN IN THE 196(

This map shows the approximate locations of the 2§
camping and retreat programs begun in the 1960§
Beginning dates and names are shown in the
chronological listing for the 1960§

■ Permanent facilities
O Improvised or leased facilities

nite Brethren, using leased facilities.

Camp Camrec, Washington, established and operated by the Washington Mennonite Fellowship of the *General Conference Mennonite Church*. Prior to Camrec, the first Junior Retreat was held in 1955 and continued each summer.

Pine Lake Fellowship Camp, Mississippi, established and operated by an association of interested persons within the *Mennonite Church*. Now operated by the Gulf States Mennonite Fellowship. Established in the interest of reconciliation of racial groups in Mississippi.

Lakewood Retreat, Florida, established and operated by an association of interested persons within the *Mennonite Church*. The camping program in the Florida churches had its beginning in 1955, using leased facilities.

1967 - **Out-Spokin'**, Indiana, a biking ministry sponsored by the *Mennonite Board of Missions*. Phased out in 1981.

Camp Keola, California, established and operated by the California Mennonite Fellowship and the *General Conference Mennonite Church*. Prior to Keola, youth camps and retreats were held in leased facilities and in cooperation with others.

Penn-York Camp, Pennsylvania, established and operated by the *Penn-York Camp Association*, an interdenominational association of interested persons. The Mennonite churches of the area provide leadership and resources.

Cove Valley Christian Youth Camp, Pennsylvania, established and operated by an association of interested persons within the *Mennonite Church*. Program emphasizes welfare camping for children from cities.

1968 - **Glenbrook Day Camp**, Ontario, sponsored by Willowgrove, an association of interested people within the *Mennonite Church*. The Willowgrove Centre is available for group use the year around. They also provide a farm program for schoolchildren from the public schools.

1969 - **Camp Seton**, Manitoba, sponsored by the Lake Winnipeg Mission Camp Society (*Mennonite Brethren*). Used by small groups for specialized programming and wilderness camping activities.

Camp Deerpark, New York, established and operated by the *Mennonite Action Program*, an inter-Mennonite project of the New York City Mennonite churches.

Beaver Camp, New York, established and operated by the

Adirondack Mennonite Camping Association, an association of interested persons from the *Mennonite churches
(MC)* of New York.

Juvenile Delinquents in Ontario

"Who will help boys who resent authority? Who will show
them that love can be honest and good and that there are loving
people? . . . Who will provide the warm loving accepting
relationship-milieu for a new and different understanding of himself to be built, through which new attitudes toward society can
evolve?" In June 1964, a letter with these questions was circulated to appeal for help with the costs of developing the facilities
of Frontier Forest Camp in Ontario. This rehabilitation program
for delinquent boys was preparing for its fifth year of operation.

The first summer in 1960, facilities adjoining Fraser Lake
Camp were used and campers ate their meals in the camp's
dining hall. Glen Brubacher and Emerson McDowell had made
successful contact with the Juvenile Court for Metro Toronto,
and had been assured that they could be supplied with all the
boys they could take. The pilot project consisted of twenty boys
for a ten-day period. The Welfare Board of the Ontario Mennonite
Conference and other interested individuals had purchased a
property specifically for this program. In 1961, when the facilities were used for the first time, there was only one cabin which
was used for the kitchen. The boys and the staff slept and ate
their meals in tents.

At the annual meeting, after the first camp had been held, the
guest speaker was Tony Barclay of the Juvenile Court. He spoke
of the need for programs such as Frontier Boys, and commented
that some of the boys had made new friends and wanted to return
again. He said, "They are children who need love and understanding." A letter of appreciation from an agency whose boys
attended Frontier Forest Camp commented, "In the past, the
agency, individual staff persons within it, and the boys have
gained immeasurably from the experience. As staff persons, we
have been inspired by the philosophy and purpose of Frontier
Camp, and by the highly motivated and dedicated people involved. The spirit of Christian love and concern permeates the
camp program, and we are convinced that this has been a central
influence in the treatment of disturbed children." God demonstrated again and again how his love can flow from dedicated
people to inspire those who know little or nothing about love and
acceptance. It was this love and the quality of staff, rather than
program technique that God was able to use in rehabilitating
lives.[2]

Year-round Resident Camp for Juvenile Delinquents in Colorado

"You as a Mennonite Church have pioneered in welfare camping. I feel that you are obligated to share what you have done with other groups. I have talked all over the country about how you Mennonites are doing this. You people have helped about 120 boys and from sixty to eighty girls and have given individual and personal service to them. You are doing a tremendous job." Thus spoke Honorable Phillip B. Gilliam, nationally known judge of the Denver Juvenile Court, at a luncheon with church leaders, camp director Jess Kauffman, and other personnel of Rocky Mountain Mennonite Camp.

The concept of peace and servanthood, as demonstrated in the lives of many persons was responsible for Judge Gilliam's evaluation. It was natural for staff persons with this background to share their love and acceptance. In turn, it was natural for those who knew little of love and acceptance to respond, but only after they were convinced that the people demonstrating this lifestyle were real and not phony.

Rocky Mountain Camp had sponsored seasonal camps for boys and girls from the courts for several summers. Some campers returned summer after summer and found this experience a source of strength during their school year back in the city. Now the staff were being challenged to begin a year-round rehabilitation program for juvenile delinquents.[3] It had been dreamed of earlier, but how could it possibly happen? Church agencies were not responsive to the idea. The support group was very small. It would require an investment in land and facilities. But God had some plans that would soon surface.

A proposed plan was written up and circulated to churches and interested individuals. The plan called for a beginning unit of fifteen boys, and a ranch-type setting in the mountains with a school, teachers, and competent staff. But that is not the way it started. It was soon after the summer program with delinquents that a call was received from Judge Gilliam that he had four boys in Juvenile Hall in Denver. He did not know what to do with them unless the camp would come and get them. One of them was reported to have set as many as twenty-five fires in Denver. Another was returned to the Denver Court after a team of psychiatrists had labeled him impossible. The other two had been back to the judge too many times for miscellaneous offenses. His final question was, "When will you be after them?"

An abandoned four-room ranch house was leased at twenty-five dollars per month. Two counselors from Rocky Mountain Camp, Ivan White and Don Headrick, volunteered their time to live with the boys. Ed and Irene Schrock organized their own support from friends and joined the staff. Jess Kauffman served as director.

That first winter in the little ranch house was not without its problems, but there were also good times. Everyone was learning. There were no servants to provide services. The boys took turns doing the cooking. Everyone, including staff, helped chop wood to keep warm, or to carry water from the spring. When weather was agreeable, days would be spent building quarters at a different location so that by summer more boys could be added.

When summer arrived, a clearing had been made on Rocky Mountain Camp property, called Frontier Ridge, and a cluster of four tent-cabins and a rustic building for a kitchen and dining hall had been constructed. New boys joined the original four. In a few months it became apparent that these facilities would not be adequate. A few miles away a private camp, complete with buildings, was offered for rent. This became the home for Frontier Boys until in the early seventies when a permanent facility was purchased at Larkspur, Colorado, and the program became known as Frontier Boys Village. It was also around this time that the Barnabas Club, the sponsoring group, decided to require all staff with administrative responsibilities to have formal training with proper degrees in social services. This meant a revamping of personnel, since the program had developed to this point without that requirement. The Frontier Boys Camp closed in 1978.

Within a couple of months after the new policies at Frontier Camp had left several staff persons without a job, the opportunity to become involved in a new program was made available. The Brockhursts at Green Mountain Falls, Colorado, owned and operated a dude ranch on their beautiful 160 acres of mountain ranch land. In their nineties, and unable to operate it, they offered their property to the local Lions Club with the stipulation that it would be used in some kind of program for boys. Jess Kauffman, a member of the local Lions Club, was asked to investigate and report the possibilities back to the club.

A trip to the agencies in Denver to announce to them what was developing was all it took to get a delegation to the ranch to investigate for themselves. A plan for developing program and policies for operation was prepared and presented at a meeting representing the various agencies in Denver who had supported the rehabilitation at both Rocky Mountain Camp and Frontier Boys Camp. They were acquainted with the programs and their success, as well as with personnel who would be directing the program.

All red tape was cut, and within thirty days the ranch was in operation with eight boys. Soon the project had outgrown a local civic club, and a foundation was formed, known as Brockhurst Foundation, which still operates the ranch (1983) with some forty boys. During its first year of operation it was staffed entirely by personnel who had worked at Rocky Mountain and Frontier Boys Camp. The same philosophy was continued, and the same response experienced, even though the program at Brockhurst Boys Ranch was designed for a boy more advanced in his antisocial behavior and attitudes.[4]

Reconciliation—The Reason for Pine Lake Fellowship Camp in Mississippi

"The reason for the camp's existence can be given in one word—*reconciliation*. And the Association's bylaws include in the purpose of the camp: 'To bring the camper into a personal living relationship with Christ and to foster growth in the Christian life, and reconciliation between racial groups in Mississippi,' " wrote Orlo Kaufman in the *Mennonite Weekly Review*. It was during the tension and violence of the 1960s that the camp was developed. "Dedication in the summer of 1968 is different. People are becoming afraid—afraid of their next-door neighbors. One radio speaker is reported to have said, 'Send us a gift to help us spread the Gospel of the saving power of Christ, and as a small token we will send you a riot gun.' The summer stretches ahead— long, hot, and violent. What does Christianity mean in a world gone crazy with fear, hate, and mistrust?"[5]

This was the South in the sixties. Racial issues involved not only black and white, but also Indians who were discriminated against and who were a subject of controversy. Many persons, both young and old, put themselves in dangerous positions when taking a stand against this injustice. The story of Nevin Bender and his involvement on behalf of the Indians is an important part of the story of Christian camping in Mississippi.

The Benders first came to Mississippi in 1959 to visit their son Titus in Meridian, Mississippi. It was during this visit that Nevin met members of the Choctaw Indian people living in the area. This aroused a long-felt desire to live and work among these people. He and his wife were deeply touched as they visited with them and sensed their needs. At the age of sixty-eight, they moved to the area and began their witness among the Indians although this was not a popular or safe thing to do in that area and at that time.

The Benders rented a house with no plumbing and their daughter and family joined them. The Nanih Waiya Mennonite Church building was completed in 1963. A year later it was bombed, and the dedication of the Benders was put to a test. With the help of friends the chapel was ready for use within a few weeks. Two years later it was bombed again. The Benders were determined to stay, and the chapel was rebuilt. That same year the house in which some of the Bender family lived was fired into six times with a high-powered rifle, and on Christmas Eve the chapel was bombed for the third time. The Benders rebuilt the chapel and stayed. In spite of all this the Benders remained true to their call to minister to the Indian people, and the congregation grew.[6]

During World War I Nevin Bender had experienced life for six months at Camp Meade as a conscientious objector, living at the army base. Since there were no provisions for conscientious objectors, he knew many times of danger and uncertainty in that situation. He both experienced and observed injustice. He saw the possibility of doing something to ease racial tensions among the Indians, blacks, and whites in the South by establishing a camp where they would have the freedom to come together for fellowship and reconciliation. When a plot of ground near Meridian became available, the Bender family provided the money to purchase it. They were assisted by others, and within a year they had organized an association for this purpose, and Pine Lake Fellowship Camp was born.

In many cases Indians, blacks, and whites are represented in the camp's activities. Its unique witness lies in the area of discipleship, peace, and Christian service. The camp has adopted the theme of reconciliation as a goal, believing that reconciliation to God and reconciliation between people are part of the same goal.

The Gulf States Mennonite Fellowship has a combined membership of 378 in nine congregations in Mississippi, Louisiana, and Alabama. They have probably the smallest support group of any of the camps in the inter-Mennonite community of camps and retreats. Those who know best the story of the camp's beginnings say that Titus Bender was the one with the dream that made it all possible.

Camping and Church Planting Team Up in Vermont

The countryside of Vermont is rich in beauty, folklore, and history. During a time of economic difficulties and changes, many of the rural people of Vermont relocated in cities or other places of employment. This often left the little rural churches without sufficient members, and the doors were closed. These empty church buildings became a concern to some people in the Franconia Mennonite Conference of Pennsylvania. Several families responded to the challenge to locate in Vermont in an effort to plant churches in these communities. One of these was the Lloyd Moyer family.

Lloyd was providing a needed service as a well driller, and this gave him many contacts with the people of the area. He was led to a 400-acre tract accessible by a winding gravel road. He dreamed of it becoming a church camp some day. Pastor Nevin Bender, Jr., of the Bethany Mennonite Church near Bridgewater Corners shared this vision with him, and this is the story behind the story of Bethany Birches Camp that is located in the scenic historic mountains of Vermont.

Rock fences, foundations of once existing buildings, and other signs tell that at one time the area had been cleared and was used for farming and grazing. The area needed clearing again of the hardhack, the brush that had taken over. Volunteers provided staff and personnel for development. Friends from the parent conference in Pennsylvania responded with money and personnel. Friends from other states became involved.

Bethany Birches is a part of the program of the three Mennonite churches in Vermont which were established during the 1950s. These pioneers in church planting were reaching out into the community and providing activities for the children. The Bethany congregation was providing an effective club program, and children and youth were being touched.

Then came those unexpected blessings. Not only was the club program at the local church strengthened as campers and friends who were not being attracted to their churches became involved. This outdoor ministry was providing these churches the opportunity to witness in a way not possible before.

A large family of the community began sending their children to the summer camp. They had one or two for every age group. Two teenage sisters attended the first week, one of whom seemed withdrawn. She did not enter into the activities with the group, but would often be observed sitting alone as if either in deep thought, or maybe depressed about something. When the week was over and the campers had returned to their homes, the staff had no way of knowing what had taken place in her life. A couple of weeks later the mother returned with more campers. She could hardly wait to share what the previous camp had meant to this daughter, and the unbelievable change that had taken place in her life. In the atmosphere of love and caring at Bethany Birches she had found God in a new way. God had become real in her life.

This story has been repeated many times as the three congregations involved in church planting team up with this outdoor ministry. The camp has enabled the Vermont Mennonite

churches to provide a ministry far beyond what their congregations could normally render.[7]

New York City Churches Consider Camping Important to Their Ministry

What had been known as Winkler's Country Club located
about eighty miles northwest of New York City in the Catskill
Mountains is now known as Camp Deerpark, owned and operated by ten churches of the Mennonite faith in New York City. For a
couple of years the several churches of the city, though representing several conferences and backgrounds, felt they could be co-
operating in some joint projects. They felt that to own and
operate a camp together was vital to their needs as a group of
churches.

The purpose of the camp would be to provide a place for the
extension of their witness and their Christian education programs. For years they had all been operating youth programs
such as work with youth on the street, in coffee shops, sandwich
shops, and youth centers. They had provided a citywide Mennonite Youth Fellowship. Now they would add to this an outdoor
ministry where their youth could experience fellowship and
Christian nurture away from their everyday world. Beyond this
they saw it as an opportunity for city youth and adult leadership
to develop relationships in this twenty-four-hour-a-day learning-
and-living experience that would be helpful as they returned to
their city environment. It was to be more than a physical retreat,
and would allow for spiritual follow-up for the inner-city programs. It was destined to become a place where entire congregations could retreat and where families could go to relax from the
pressures of their city life.

Mennonite Action Program, Inc., was established with a board
of directors for the purpose of purchasing, developing, and
operating Camp Deerpark. The buildings that came with the
original purchase of the 280 acres, sixty of which were cleared,
were ready for use for their first summer of camping in 1969.
Expansion of facilities and remodeling to meet the needs of a
growing program and the requirements of the state came later.
From the very beginning it was the concern that the people of the
churches would feel that it was their camp and their project, and
not a facility that some other person or group had provided them.
The youth were to feel that they had a part in it also, and that it
was theirs because they had helped. Funds were provided by
Mennonite Central Committee to hire eleven youth from the city
for several weeks to assist in the camp's operation. Some of these
fellows were ex-addicts from the Center who had become Chris-

tians. Inner-city youth continued to be used in development and trained for leadership in camping. Congregations were soon reserving the camp for retreats and were planning their programs and providing leadership.

It is significant that 80 percent of the youth campers at Deerpark are from nonchurch or non-Christian homes. Because of this outdoor ministry they have expanded their ministry to hundreds of youth whom they would not have touched in their city programs. It has been a beautiful example of churches from varying backgrounds and conferences uniting in this ministry. The program has contributed to fellowship of these churches within the city who have come to know each other in a way that would have been impossible had it not been for Camp Deerpark.[8]

Wilderness Camping—Welfare Camps—at Pennsylvania Spruce Lake Camp

"We pitched our tents, and watched God work. As we drove out Wilderness Road we could not help but praise God for his presence during another camping season. We had seen him at work in so many ways, and often felt his presence." This was the way Al Detweiler expressed his sentiments, and then added, "As we thought back over the summer, we could recall so vividly the day we had driven this same road with the first carloads of robust campers to start our camping program for the summer."

The camping program in the Franconia Mennonite Conference began taking shape in the late 1940s. In the spring of 1949 leadership in the Allentown Mennonite Church saw the need for a camp experience for the youth of the city who were attending their church activities. The first year of camp was one week for fifty campers. For the next fifteen years the conference used the facilities of Men-O-Lan for the Allentown church camping program. In 1951 the Young People's Committee of the conference sponsored two weeks of camping for the mission churches. As the ministry of camping grew, the conference named Al Detweiler to serve as director of the camping ministry. The expansion of this program led to the development of Spruce Lake Retreat in the Pocono Mountains of northeastern Pennsylvania. This would serve adult and family groups, and a 240-acre tract one mile away, the Spruce Lake Wilderness Camp, was designed for children and youth.

In 1960 the report in the *Mission News* for Franconia Conference read, "The camping program for our mission church youth has added the tenth chapter to the history of welfare camping of the Franconia conference. . . . This was a good growing season for vegetables and fruits, and the Lord blessed the camp with liberal donations of beans, corn, tomatoes, watermelons, apples, and peaches. Most of the meat and poultry were donated by individuals. Liberal offerings from Sunday schools and congregations were received for the support of the program."

Coed camping was introduced in the early 1970s, and the camping program was to include all the mission churches of the Franconia Conference. Camping for underprivileged and emotionally handicapped youth has been recognized as an important ministry at Spruce Lake Wilderness Camp from its beginning, as well as the camping ministry that preceded Spruce Lake's development. Al Detweiler has given continued leadership to this program, starting as director in 1956, and with a dedicated staff from summer to summer had developed one of the unique programs in our community of camps and retreats. An indication of its success is contained in this report: "The beginning of the miracle during youth camp began on Monday evening when about half out of ninety-two campers and many of the staff had rededicated their lives to Jesus Christ. Many that were not Christians came to know the Lord as their personal Saviour. By the time the week ended there were very few campers that had not made some kind of new commitment of their lives to the Lord."[9]

Out-Spokin'—The Unique Contribution to the Outdoor Ministry

Whether biking or hiking, the ministry sponsored by the Mennonite Board of Missions challenged and changed the lives of many persons, young and old. The dream child of Terry Burkhalter, Out-Spokin' enjoyed fifteen years of biking and hiking across the country. Participants ranged in age from six to seventy-eight. Trips covering much of North America, Jamaica, and Europe lasted from one day to two months. Backpacking trips varied from short trips to extended ones in areas such as the Great Smoky Mountains and the Glacier National Park.

"How does biking change lifestyles? Mix together twenty-four completely different people who will need to work together as a team, whether they like it or not. Add unavoidable circumstances like extreme physical stress, the unbiased whims of chance and mother nature, and the human experiences of confrontation and cooperation along with consolation and celebration. Add devotional input regarding the differences between being a Christian and not being one. Mix for seven weeks, and allow God to work." This was the comment of Les Engle, devotional leader for the 1976 coast-to-coast trip that started at Lincoln City, Oregon, and culminated at Hampton Beach, New Hampshire, some 3,800 miles and seven weeks later.[10]

It all started in 1967 when Terry Burkhalter was attending school at Malone College. As a part-time youth sponsor, he would bike with the youth of the John Knox Presbyterian Church in Canton, Ohio, on weekends. He had also become acquainted with Coach Bob Davenport of Taylor University, Upland, Indiana, who had organized a biking program known as Wandering Wheels. The idea of an extended bike trip began to play in Terry's mind. He teamed up with Dewayne Johns and others and the dream became reality. Soon the program was in need of a wider base of support. When the Mennonite Mission Board was approached, they referred the project to Ray Horst, secretary for Relief and Service, and his belief and enthusiasm for the program and its potential was instrumental in giving it this support.

Was Out-Spokin' to be considered a recreational program only, or would it have other values built into it? Would it be providing an activity that only the rich could afford, or could it include all young people? These were the kinds of questions being asked as the program struggled in its beginning. But the vision of Terry and others, along with the experiences of the bikers, soon provided positive answers to these concerns. They saw it as a potential for bringing young people together in a group experience under supervision, with input and guidance for sharing, studying, and growing together. These goals were all realized, along with other values, such as the exposure to nature and its elements. Sometimes it was too wet, or too cold, or too hot. Maybe they were riding into a head wind; maybe the wind was to their backs and helping them along. The grades could be long and steep, but coasting down the other side was a reward. Coping with these varied conditions was part of the process that contributed to growth. This was the only outdoor ministry of the church that limited its activities to biking or hiking, although several of the camps provided these experiences as a part of their program.

It was in 1970 that Jerry Miller became involved as its director. The program had grown to a four-season operation. Its staff had grown from a summer voluntary service unit to a full-time staff of four. Jerry did not direct the program from an armchair in his office. He was often on a bicycle with the group. He wanted to experience all that the bikers were feeling, so that he would be able to relate to them and their problems. He and his wife, Becky, gave beyond the call of duty in those beginning days, as both of them worked full time on a half-time basis and salary.

After fifteen years and after over 10,000 bikers had logged nearly 2½ million rider miles, the program was phased out by the Mission Board. Out-Spokin' is only a memory now, but a very dear one to many persons. The program was conceived out of a concern for youth in the turbulent sixties. It grew out of the vision of youth, and it was their enthusiasm and leadership that got it on the road. Commenting about God at work in the Out-Spokin' program, Jerry said, "I saw miracles, some little and some big, in the lives of persons. I saw a caring community, uniting in a common cause. People from varying backgrounds and value systems came together and formed a community with love and caring for one another.[11]

Three Men—Their Visions—and Their Farm

In 1968 Emerson McDowell, Nicholas Dick, and Glen Brubaker purchased a ninety-two-acre farm near Markham, Ontario, that had been in the Grove family for 168 years. They incorporated as Willowgrove Farm Ltd. In a brief history of Willowgrove, written by J. M. Nighswander for the 1982 annual meeting he shared some of the visions these three men had to put the farm into production for the Lord:

> I can remember very clearly the verbal sparring which was a regular feature of their meetings as plans, policies, procedures, programs, and problems were hammered out through vigorous and emphatic dialogue! I used to say it was the highlight of my month in terms of entertainment. Emerson saw the farm and its programs in operation primarily to serve city children. He saw Willowgrove as a setting where children could learn wholesome values, and where they could experience the love of God as expressed in nature and through the lives of the staff. He also saw the farm as a resource for retirement. Nicholas saw the farm more as a retreat for Mennonites from the city, where they could grow gardens, do weekend camping, and perhaps where a retirement community could be built in the future. He had dreams of creating a Mennonite center where history could be displayed and preserved. Glen perceived the farm as a place where boys who were having problems could experience the love and care of responsible people, where they could understand perhaps for the first time the security of a family, and where the touch of nature and the great outdoors could bring healing to hurting minds and emotions.

A statement of purpose written early in Willowgrove's history reads: "It is the objective of Willowgrove to create settings where community and brotherhood can be experienced, and where healthy primary human relationships can be developed in children and young people. . . . Its purpose is to assist individuals, families and groups to develop a sense of personal worth, community spirit, service to mankind, and to appreciate the world in which we live."

A program known as Glenbook Day Camp began in 1969. The first summer they reported 300 camper weeks; and by 1982 that many campers were attending each day, for a period of nine weeks each summer. Children ages five through twelve are transported by two large busses and fourteen vans. Facilities include a large barn for recreation, a large building that can be heated for games on rainy days, facilities for sports such as tennis, swimming, baseball, and skating. There is a team of Belgian horses for the sled, and tractor and wagon for hayrides. A farm with all the animals completes the setting.

"We have one camper here today whom we could not account for," wrote Director Rachel Schmucker in her daily log. "He is about six or seven years old and the phone number he gave us contacts his Chinese grandmother who only speaks her own language. This afternon we put him on the bus, and finally at 6:30 I reached his mother by phone who laughed and said he was to have gotten on the school bus and gone to his French class; but that he really enjoyed his day at camp."[12]

Willowgrove Group Home was opened in 1968 with Eldo and Rosa Toews as houseparents. Boys were referred by the Children's Aid Societies and Metro Social Services. Up to six boys could be accommodated. The farmhouse was used as the boys' home. The boys were in residence from several months to one year or more, and attended the public schools of the area. The basic purpose of the program was to provide a community service that would keep the boys out of the Training School. After providing a residence for many boys where there was love and healing, the home was terminated in 1982 due to changes in government policies that affected its continuation.

The Willowgrove Outdoor Education Program was begun in 1976, with the objective of providing city children a farm experience where they could become aware of the farm and its animals and natural environment. Over 10,000 children tour the farm each year. The brochure describing the program refers to it as a classroom in the country: "Shaking straw out of your shirt, riding a tractor-drawn wagon and figuring out what a goat likes to eat are part of the Willowgrove experience. The 92-acre farm has a year-round stream, a mature woodlot and a large barn which houses various farm animals. Upstairs in the haymow, children can jump and play in the hay and swing from the beams in safety."

Any season of the year is a good time for children to enjoy the farm and its program. In the fall they are invited to the garden where they can pick some vegetables to take back to their classroom. In October they can go to the pumpkin patch and get a pumpkin for their classroom's jack-o-lantern. In December they get a sleigh ride or help decorate the Christmas tree. During the colder winter months they skate and toboggan. In March they help tap the maple trees and boil down the sap; and in the spring they go to the woodlot and observe the spring flowers. Outdoor education of this kind has been included in the ministry of several of our camps, but not in the same dimension and with the excitement of Willowgrove.

The Willowgrove Centre is described as a peaceful retreat in the woods. Its primary function is to provide an informal setting for groups to meet for recreation, fellowship and study, and to offer worthwhile programs for children, youth, and adults. The center is available the year-round for a variety of group uses. These include churches and community events, group retreats, recreation experiences, and a day-camping program.

Stories of Cooperation Among the Mennonite Brethren

The story of camping in the Mennonite Brethren Church is not complete by limiting it to only church-owned campsites. In addition to establishing thirteen campsites in Canada and three in the United States, Mennonite Brethren have cooperated in the establishment of campsites with other evangelical churches, and own and operate them as a cooperative adventure. Typical of these is Camp Loma De Vida in the Latin American District in south Texas. This is an example of evangelical Christians working together to make a program possible that neither of them could accomplish alone. Each group is benefiting from the use of the camp and its facilities, and using it to expand its ministry of missions and evangelism. Yet it is not counted as one of the Mennonite Brethren Camps.

Camp Oshkidee in Saskatchewan is a part of the story of Mennonite Brethren camping; yet it was neither owned nor directly related to the church. Christian Service Brigade and Pioneer Girls organizations have been common among the Mennonite Brethren. When a camp was needed to promote these programs effectively, the Jeanette Lake Camping Association was formed to purchase land and develop facilities. The Mennonite Brethren and other evangelical groups with similar concerns pooled their efforts, and everyone benefited. A number of other camps have been organized to permit other Christians to be involved in ownership and operation of the program and development. In this respect the camps are interdenominational, at least in operation.

Unique to the Mennonite Brethren program is the active camping and retreat movement in the Southern and Central districts of the United States conferences. Because the districts are large, and the churches scattered, getting people together is difficult. Neither district has a church-owned campsite, yet both have been very active and successful in promoting camps for their youth, adults, and families, beginning as early as the 1940s. The Pacific District has established Hartland Bible Camp, but only after an active camping program had been established. The North Carolina District is small in number, but also has an active camping program for their youth, which was begun in the early 1940s. All five of the Mennonite Brethren districts in the United States have active camping programs with a total of hundreds of participants each summer. Camping is considered one of the forces that has inspired youth to loyalty to the church and the motivation to enter Christian service.

CHAPTER SEVEN

The Seventies

A Decade with New Opportunities,
More Expansion,
Another Generation

The Seventies saw the camps enlarging,
winterizing, expanding programs
to include more groups,
programs for the handicapped,
ethnic and minority groups.
Camping had found its way
into the mainstream of church life
and Christian education.

Several decades ago the camping movement was compared to a grain of mustard seed. The beginnings were small, but over the years the camping movement in the Mennonite and Brethren in Christ community of camps and retreats has grown steadily. The program has proven its worth and is making its contribution in Christian education and evangelism.

Ten new facilities were added during the period from 1970 to 1982. Camps and retreat centers that had previously existed were in many cases enlarging, winterizing, expanding programs to include more groups and interests, and making their facilities available to other churches on a rental basis. Many were including programs for the physically and emotionally handicapped, as well as for ethnic and minority groups. Camps and programs that were originally designed for youth during the summer months were often winterized and included facilities for adult groups and families. Coed camping had become the accepted practice. Programs that were originally tailored for the children and youth of the church were finding themselves including many children from their communities in which they were located. Many camps were reporting a ratio of Mennonite to non-Mennonite or unchurched campers as much as fifty-fifty. Friendship evangelism was apparent as campers brought friends with them, often those who later would attend the functions of the traditional church.

The 1970s were important to development and expansion. It was not a time when progress could be put on hold to see what might happen next. Bradford Sears, a nationally known camp consultant made this statement at the beginning of the decade, "The church must either decide that the spiral of evolution is going to lead to the phasing out of camps and retreats; or it must take a bold look at innovative, exciting, new programs and facilities that speak to today's and tomorrow's world and make the major investment gamble that these programs demand. If staffed with first-rate leadership, and operated in facilities that are models for others to follow, we will have something of lasting value to offer in the work of the church." In this decade many daring adventures and investments were made within the community of camps and retreat centers.

Another interesting trend is the fact that each summer there is more competition, more activities bidding for the camper-age youth. Specialized camps in sports and technology, including computer camps, causes the potential camper to take another look at the traditional church camp and this challenges camping staffs to keep programs relevant to the needs and interests of youth. In spite of these challenges, attendance has remained stable.

The development of new facilities was leveling off. Expansion and improvements were usually to make existing facilities more functional, rather than add to the number of camps. Those camps located in a density of population, or near a cluster of churches, were experiencing growth in the number and variety of activities they were able to host. Supporting churches, as well as other interest groups, had discovered the value of these facilities for supplementing their programs and interests. The growing need for facilities where small groups could retreat accounted for much of this growth.

The outdoor ministry was opening up new approaches to evangelism as well as providing the opportunity for many young people to become involved in a program of outreach and friendship evangelism. Thousands of youth had served as cabin leaders and support staff over the years. Many adults had the opportunity to experience Christian service through the camping program. J. B. Toews in this history of the Mennonite Brethren says, "The spiritual impact of the Christian camps on the young people in our communities can hardly be overestimated. Often when congregations hear the testimonies of baptismal candidates, they hear accounts of our young people who experienced conversion or renewal of commitment to Christ while attending a Christian camp."[1]

Significant Beginnings in the 1970s

1970 - **Harman Mountain Farm Campground**, West Virginia, established by the *Central District Virginia Mennonite Conference (MC)*. Operated for tourist campers and family gatherings

1971 - **Camp Oshkidee**, Saskatchewan, sponsored by the Jeanette Lake Camping Association. *Mennonite Brethren* relate to the camp with their Christian Service Brigade and Pioneer Girls programs.
    Ryerson Bible Camp, Ontario, owned by the United Church and leased by the *Mennonite Brethren* when they moved their camping program from Eden Bible School to a camp setting. The camping program moved from here to Oak-A-Lea in 1975.

1972 - **Outbound Camping Program**, Saskatchewan, sponsored by the *Conference of Mennonites of Saskatchewan (GC)*. Owns equipment only and sponsors canoe camps, backpacking, cycling camps.

1973 - **Camp Andrews**, Pennsylvania, established by the Baltimore Mennonite Mission of the *Lancaster Mennonite Conference (MC)*. Works primarily with city children.

1974 - **Gardom Lake Bible Camp**, British Columbia, owned by the *Mennonite Brethren*, but operated by an inter-denominational board of ten churches of the area.
Camp Peniel, Quebec, a *Mennonite Brethren* camp serving French-speaking people.
Spring Lake Retreat, New York, owned and operated by the *Brethren in Christ*. Serves children from New York City and Brethren in Christ churches.

1975 - **Zenith Camp of the Ozarks**, Arkansas, a *private camp* operated by the Ray Stutzman family. Also a foster home for children.
Simonhouse Bible Camp, Manitoba, sponsored by the Manitoba Home Missions Committee of the *Mennonite Brethren Church*. Programs for youth, families, wilderness camping and backpacking.
Oak-A-Lea, Ontario, a privately owned campsite leased by the *Mennonite Brethren* prior to their purchase of Crossroads.

1976 - **Pembina Valley Camp**, Manitoba, an extension of Winkler Bible Camp. The additional acreage was secured by the *Mennonite Brethren* for expansion and a future retreat center. Now used for wilderness camping.

1978 - **Christian Retreat Center**, Pennsylvania, developed and operated by the *Brethren in Christ Church*, Allegheny Conference. Programs for all ages.

1979 - **Shekinah Retreat Centre**, Saskatchewan, developed and operated by the *General Conference Mennonite Church*. Replaced Pike Lake Bible Camp which was founded in 1956.

1980 - **Merry Lea Environmental Center**, Indiana, established by Lee and Mary Jane Reith in the middle 1960s, and given to *Goshen College*, Goshen, Indiana, to preserve and use as a natural habitat and for environmental education.
Camp Crossroads, Ontario, established by the Ontario Conference of the *Mennonite Brethren Church*. In 1973 the official name for the Ontario Mennonite Brethren Camps became "Camp Crossroads." Prior to this, camping programs had been held at Eden, Ryerson, and Oak-A-Lea.
Crooked Creek Christian Camp, Iowa, established by the *Southeast Iowa Mennonite Camping Association*, representing the inter-Mennonite community of churches in Iowa.

1982 - **Lifecyclin'**, Virginia, sponsored by the *Virginia Menno-*

MENNONITE CAMPING PROGRAMS BEGUN IN THE 1970s

This map shows the approximate location of the 16
camping and retreat programs begun in the 1970s.
Beginning dates and names are shown in the
chronological listing for the 1970s.

■ Permanent facilities
O Improvised or leased facilities

nite Conference (MC) Youth Office. A spin-off of Out-Spokin' bike program founded in 1967, with the purchase of Out-Spokin' equipment.

A beginning of a Different Sort—Gardom Lake Bible Camp

Gardom Lake Bible Camp is a gift to the young. One day in the early 1970s Oswald Dobell, a retired farmer, was strolling over his acreage on the shores of Gardom Lake, near Enderby, British Columbia. He began thinking of it in relation to youth. How could he make it available so that it could benefit them? His dream was to see the property remain uncommercialized and in some way provide an alternative to the concerns that young people felt so strongly during the 1960s. Maybe he could give it to someone who would use it in this way, perhaps a church. Somehow the news got around and Jake Balzer, minister of the Valleyview Mennonite Brethren Church, heard of it. He called his friend, Nick Dyck, director of church extension, and they visited the property. Finding that it had the potential for an ideal camp, Balzer made his initial contact with Dobell, and expressed the interest in Mennonite Brethren establishing a camp for youth.

Who were these people who were interested? Dobell wondered. By 1972 Dobell had checked out the Mennonites. He found them to be honest and hardworking people, religious, and known to aid the needy and care for their youth. Dobell called Jake for another meeting. This led to a meeting with the Mennonite Brethren Conference Board of Management. In 1974 an agreement, worked out by Dobell and the conference lawyer, was signed.[2]

Even though the agreement stipulated that Gardom Lake should always remain the property of the Mennonite Brethren, it did not forbid other Christian fellowships from becoming a part of the program. Other churches of the area were invited to participate in the development and program. The camp is operated by a board representing ten churches, three Mennonite Brethren, and other evangelical congregations of the area. This board has total jurisdiction of the camp's operation. Balzer, who remains the chairman (1981) is always optimistic. "We do not think in terms of denominations. We think in terms of a place where people are helped and God is truly honored. We think of it as sort of a guiding point for many in the Okanagan Valley." Jake continues, "I am convinced that God is in this thing. And, in turn, we want to honor God on these grounds."[3]

The Outdoor Ministry Takes on Varied Forms

The decade of the 1970s saw expansion in various ways. The Central District Virginia Conference of the Mennonite Church sensed a need for facilities for families and church groups that could best be provided in an outdoor setting. A farm of 122 acres was purchased at Harman, West Virginia, and a portion of it used for a campground where families, church groups, and tourist campers could come for fellowship and worship in a Christian environment. A pavilion, bathhouse, and recreational equipment are provided. Guests are encouraged to be creative and restful in their activities. The pastor of one of the local congregations lives at the farm and directs the program of the campground.

In Baltimore, Maryland, the people at the Baltimore Mennonite Mission had the vision of utilizing an outdoor setting to enhance their ministry. The mission had provided a center in the city where youth and their parents could come and find someone who cared about them. They sensed the need for something beyond the frustrations of the city. God led them to a wooded property which they purchased. "Here children and teens escape the inner-city environment. They leave the concrete and its broken glass behind them to enjoy the refreshing beauty of grass and trees with a stream to wade in. A whole new picture of God's goodness and greatness is possible through the enjoyment of nature and meditating on the meaning of life and God's design for them. Meaningful times of sharing God's word has enriched their camping experience."[4] They named it Camp Andrews, getting their inspiration for the name from the admirable characteristics of Andrew, the apostle.

In the Ozark mountains of Arkansas, sparsely inhabited with country folks, the Ray Stutzman family was moved to establish a small camp setting on their farm where children could come for a period of a few days to experience life in another way with their friends, where there would be fellowship and Bible study, as well as recreation and fun. It operated as a private camp, known as Zenith Camp of the Ozarks. Friends from neighboring congregations provided support in constructing buildings and in staffing the program. It also provides a foster home for children.

The Merry Lea Environmental Center at Wolf Lake, Indiana, was given to Goshen College, Goshen, Indiana, by its founders, Lee and Mary Jane Reith, to use as a natural habitat and environmental education. The Center is used for day camping, visits by groups and schools, nature study, and silent sports such as hiking, birdwatching, and cross-country skiing. Snowmobiling and off-the-road vehicles are prohibited. Merry Lea is being managed as a large, relatively undisturbed sanctuary for the native plants and animals. Hunting and camping disrupt this natural development, and are not included in their program.

The Conference of Mennonites of Saskatchewan organized the Outbound Program, whose purpose is to offer an alternative camping experience that is more challenging and physically demanding than the conventional camp. In the Christian context the campers are to be made aware of God, of themselves, of the stewardship of creation, and of caring for each other, as they travel, work, study, and live together as a small group where living is reduced to simple dimensions. The program includes canoe trips, backpacking camps, and cycling camps. The program does not include facilities, but equipment only.

Pembina Valley Camp, founded by the Mennonite Brethren of Manitoba, is an extension of Winkler Bible Camp. Its 240 acres lend themselves to wilderness camping, and complements Winkler's program of away-from-camp activities. These recent efforts to encourage this dimension of a camping experience strengthen the existing programs of many of the camps across the country which are providing similar experiences.

Consolidating, enlarging, and replacing camp and retreat facilities was a trend of the 1970s. Shekinah Retreat Centre, Waldheim, Saskatchewan, was founded by the Conference of Mennonites of Saskatchewan to replace Pike Lake Bible Camp that had been established in 1956. The Mennonite Brethren of Ontario established Camp Crossroads to replace and consolidate their outdoor ministry which had been held at Eden, Ryerson, and Oak-A-Lea over a period of nearly thirty years. In Iowa the community of inter-Mennonite congregations organized to establish a camp and retreat center known as Crooked Creek Christian Camp near Washington, Iowa. The development of the facilities is to encourage and make possible the development of a program of camps and retreats.

The establishment of Simonhouse Bible Camp, Cranberry Portage, Manitoba, by the Manitoba Mennonite Brethren Conference was motivated by an interest in missions and church planting, as well as belief in outdoor ministry as an effective form of evangelism. When the Home Missions Committee began making plans for a ministry in northern Manitoba, camping was a part of the original design. A two-fold mission was projected: the development of community-centered churches, and a strong camping ministry. A Christian day camp was started immediately, with the resident camp to follow as an extension of the congregation being established.

Un tete a tete avec Dieu (a one to one with God) is the title of an article promoting Camp Peniel of Quebec, a camp established for the French-speaking people of the Mennonite Brethren churches of Quebec. Located north of Montreal at Laurel, Quebec, Camp

Peniel combines activities such as hiking and skiing with a strong evangelistic emphasis.

CHAPTER EIGHT

Mennonite Camping: A Legacy to Cherish

Camping is people . . .

It is people with needs —
and people with determination
to grow in their
understanding and
relationship with God
and each other . . .

Sometimes it is people who are struggling
with values
and direction for life . . .

And, sometimes it is people
who resist and reject
the abundant life
that could be theirs through Jesus Christ . . .
Perhaps they are experimenting with moral values;
experiencing defeat and frustration . . .

But all are people — people who are searching
people who have a faith to share
and people who want to listen and grow . . .

And that is why there are Christian camps!
to provide a place with
an atmosphere
and a program
where there can be renewal,
discovery,
commitment,
and a return to the live-a-day world
with strength and purpose for living.

— written for the Friedenswald Staff Manual, 1972

Stories and Potpourri

When asked by his pastor whether he had given his heart to Jesus, a little boy replied, "No, I haven't been to camp yet." —related by the late Rev. Ed Lautermilch of Saskatchewan.

Little Jimmie returned from camp, and his parents were quizzing him about what had happened at camp. Among other questions they asked, "Did you get homesick?"

"No, but some of the kids did," he replied. "Especially the ones with dogs."

High in the Colorado Rockies a group of campers and their counselors were sitting around a small campfire. They had been backpacking for several days. For devotions the counselor was using the verse, "Behold I stand at the door and knock."

One of the fellows spoke up and said, "That's exactly how I feel. Man, I feel beat inside. I feel like I'm in a little box six inches square that is full of ants, and can't get out. I wish I could take a knife and cut my heart out and take it down to the stream and wash it!" This was the beginning of a new life for him.

Camp Hebron has a Plus-60 camp for campers from the inner city. One lady, eighty-two, came to camp limping, using a cane. After a few days she didn't need her cane, and her limp had improved. Another camper, seventy, immediately took off her shoes when she arrived, walked over the grass to the middle of the playing field, and stood there crying. She said she was overwhelmed with all the beauty and the feel of grass under her feet. It had been twenty years since this had happened to her.

A pastor reflects: A lad makes an altar from a rustic chair and is born from above. A lassie discovers the joy of fellowship and prayer, and sets a pattern for her life. An older youth gives a week as counselor, testing the dynamics of fundamental relationships. Away from the polite, polished, and pretended circumstances, comes to grip with the basic meaning of the Christian life and witness. Wiser, more aware of Christ, these people return to us. Quietly, like vitamins injected into tired blood, they make their contribution at the growing edge of the church.
—Fraser Lake Camp

We had some problems with homesickness. One bad case of homesickness and fear of the dark came to a sudden end on a

Friday night when the cabin discovered a family of mice had moved in with them. They moved into the basement of the lodge and went to sleep.
—Camp Amigo

Jimmy Roberts, Cove Valley Christian Camp, made the front page of the *Hagerstown Daily Mail*. Under Jimmy's picture was the caption, "Boy on High Street starts an ecology cleanup program." He had initiated a community cleanup in the lower income neighborhood where he lived by getting all the boys on his street to pick up the paper and junk off the street. He had gotten the idea at camp. During his camping experience he was required to clean up the cabin one morning by himself because he had been delinquent in helping. The director adds, "We hope Jimmy learned many more things at camp."

The swamp hike at Camp Friedenswald was popular for a number of years. Campers would follow their leaders as they followed the trail across the swamp, wading as much as waist deep in the mixture of water, vegetation, and muck. The girls dared their mothers to do it when they went to Women's Retreat in the fall. Wading through a swamp filled with muck and encountering other little creatures who make it their home is not an experience to anticipate, but a group of these mothers came prepared and walked through the swamp.

A camper wrote home, "We put a cup of water above the door. When the counselor came in, he got wet. Thanks for the cookies. Bye now."

Counselor Nancy Yost shares her observations: "It is hard to put my feelings on paper about Deerpark. They are feelings that have enriched my life so deeply and so positively they will never be erased. . . . I can remember sitting on the porch watching the bus unload. I unconsciously guarded my own thoughts and feelings so that the actions and looks of the picture I was beholding wouldn't distort my goals and intentions. As I looked through the black of each eye there was fear, distrust, wonder, and perhaps a bit of wavering belief as they surveyed the green grass which led their eyes to the woods and mountains beyond."

"There was considerable sickness in this group and the doctor had to come several times. There were several cases of severe sore throat and fever, a heart attack, an appendicitis attack, and stomach disorders. There were several experiences with wood ticks." From Tel-Hai in the early camps with city children.

"Dear Mom and Dad: We are going to have a bonfire tonight, and I am in it. That's all, goodbye."

A group of campers and their counselor had spent the week at Round Lake at an out-post camp. Before returning to the base camp on the assigned day, they decided that it would be nice to have a communion service as a last memory. They lacked all the necessary ingredients, but that did not stop them. They dug up a sassafras root, boiled some tea, and found a few broken crackers that were left over. A meaningful experience resulted.

Georgia had come to camp as a welfare camper from Denver. It was a totally new experience for her. After she had been at camp several days she shared this: "It was while I was attending the services on Sunday morning that this happened to me. It seemed as if I was in a heavy fog, and while a prayer was being prayed, a little hole appeared in the fog and I could see light. It was like being in a dark cave, and all at once seeing light. You will never know how much Rocky Mountain Camp has meant to me. It has changed my entire outlook on life. In fact, it is the first time in my life that I have had a favorable impression of the church and religion."

Gene had been at camp the previous summer. When he returned he asked, "Are we going to have church tomorrow? I enjoy church at camp. But I will need to find another thinking spot." Gene was one of the campers referred by the juvenile court, and it was the practice of some of them to have thinking spots. These were secret places where they would go alone, or maybe take a trusted friend. His had been a large rock in the stream, and in some development this had been removed.

Jeff was one of those campers who caused problems with the counselor, the campers, and everyone with whom he came in contact. One day, to everyone's surprise, one of the campers came to the director with the information that Jeff was down in his cabin and wanted to be saved. The counselors and his cabin group went to their cabin to find Jeff. The campers prayed too, and one said, "Get ready, God, here comes Jeff!"

Money for camp development was always hard to come by. Highland Camp was having an auction of goods that had been donated. A goat came on the block. Bidding was brisk, and the goat brought an inflated price. The new owner promptly donated the goat to the organization to sell again. Again the goat brought a fantastic price. Six times this goat went up for sale. When the sale ended, Highland Retreat was $200 better off.

In 1945 the Illinois churches sponsored a camp for boys in leased facilities. The fee for going to camp was five dollars and a half pound of sugar. (During World War II sugar was rationed to families, and camps could not get any.)

"The first day in Camp Squeah kitchen was long and hot. Fourteen hours long. The pies were in the oven too long—the stove had stopped working. There were not enough potatoes, and instant ones were stirred up as the campers marched in. No one remembered to put water in the freezer and we drank warm water for dinner. The chicken was a bit tough; the stove had gone out again. While handling the heavy pots I thought how easy it would be to get scalded. Should it happen, what a good excuse to go home. But it didn't and I stayed. The stove was repaired. We remembered to have ice. The weather cooled down a bit. Each day was better. It was a good week. In our kitchen we put up a poster that said, 'Nothing's rough enough to make me complain.' It really worked. Praise God." —One of the cooks at Camp Squeah.

"Campers and staff have gone home, but camp is not over. It will not be over until campers forget the love that was shown to them in various ways. They must never forget. Some campers also learned about and experienced for themselves the Source of True Love as they took Jesus to be their Savior and friend. . . . Once again, thanks, and as you serve Christ daily, I know that you will experience the peace and joy that only he can give." A letter from a Fraser Lake board member to the staff of the summer.

At 5:00 p.m. the phone rang at the office of Rocky Mountain Camp. The caller said: "This is Harold Jones. Could you possibly squeeze in just one more boy? Orville has just asked me for the sixteenth time, 'Why didn't I get to go back to camp with the other guys yesterday?' "
Orville was at camp by noon the next day to join the other guys

in a backpacking trip and a work camp. It was the beginning of a new chapter for his life. He was off the street. His episodes with Juvenile Court were over. He was a repeat camper for several summers, and then on the staff. He continued to be a leader among his peers, the same as when he was on the street. But now his leadership had taken a new direction. It was positive and constructive.

Those Wonderful People Known As Volunteers

The story of the camping movement is one of people helping people. More often than not there was no money to pay people for their services. Most of the development and programming has been done by volunteers over the years. There were the people on the boards who not only contributed days of time, but also drove hundreds of miles at their own expense, put their signatures on notes when borrowing money, made important decisions, and sometimes wrote checks on their personal accounts. Others were involved in the development of the camps. They came with their hammers and bulldozers. Shovels, picks, axes, chain saws, machetes—all were needed. Tractors and horses and wagons were involved. These were used by men and women and youth as camps and retreat centers became reality. Teachers and preachers and teenagers; college and career people, housewives and mothers, farmers and merchants—everyone became a part of the drama. Youth groups and congregations, young and old, became involved in construction of buildings, planting trees, clearing areas, cooking, cleaning, painting. Each one was multiplying the vision of the founders in his or her own unique way. Like the instruments of an orchestra, it takes many working together in harmony to produce music. Some brought materials along with them when donating their time, and then somehow the camp did not receive a bill for either the materials or services. Others who could not be involved in work projects were supporting the program with their prayers and encouragement. As in the enactment of a drama there were those who were unseen, those working behind the scenes, but equally important.

Tracie is symbolic of these beautiful people. She was at Camp Friedenswald each summer for several years. Each summer when she left she would say, "If my get-up and go hasn't gone, I'll be back next summer." Tracie was in her eighties. Campers loved her, and would have a party for her when she left for her home. When they wanted a picture of her out at the end of the high dive she accommodated them. Outside the dining hall was a clump of roses known as Tracie's roses. She planted them there, and each summer they received her loving care. She fed them banana peels to make them smell fragrant. She loved practical jokes and was often the aggressive one. Every once in a while something clever would appear on the bulletin board, and it was probably Tracie who put it there.

Of course Tracie never wanted anything for her services, but one time some cash was placed in her purse. After she returned to her home she sent this letter: "At this moment I can no longer put off having a little chat with you. First I want to thank you for the support someone put in my purse. I hope I can do something in return. This past summer was really one to remember. The staff was one of the best. I have been telling the folks here that this was my best summer yet. I am glad I could give my time and love to camp this summer. But with all the kindness and living with the group, I am sure I received more than I gave." Thank God for so many other Tracie Rabers that have made the camping ministry so fruitful.

It was in the early 1950s. Camping in the Mennonite church was relatively new, and did not have the support of the masses. It was taking a hard sell to convince many persons that this out-door ministry was an extension of the church. A group of camp leaders were discussing techniques of promotion. Little Eden in Michigan had become successful as a family camp. The group began to pick the manager's brain. How do you do it? Some persons who had been guests at the camp shared little bits of information, most of which related to courtesies on the part of the manager. The group concluded that what was needed was more Harley Nofzigers. Harley was the manager. Thank God for all these persons who have volunteered their services and given this kind of plus to the ministry of camping.

The list of miracles would be lengthy if all the times when God gave someone the urge to donate time and skills at just the right time were known and recorded. Rocky Mountain Camp was about to open for the second summer. After starting with only primitive facilities, a bathhouse was a must. A plumber was needed, but hiring was entirely out of the question. There was a knock at the door of the director's residence. A stranger announced that he was a plumber and was available to spend a few weeks at the camp if there was anything he could do. God knew exactly where to send him. He had driven nearly 2,000 miles. Thank God for Ben Kauffman, and all the other "Bens" across the camps of North America. It would not have happened without you.

It is nothing short of a miracle how God has chosen volunteers with all the skills needed in this outdoor ministry; whether it was for development and construction, or for programming. This multitude of persons has been responsible in a large measure for the very existence of this outdoor ministry.

A Tribute to the Women in the Movement

The story of Mennonite camping would not be complete without a recognition of the important role women played in its formative years. Camping was a thing for men and boys until the turn of the twentieth century. Before that it was considered neither safe or appropriate for young women with good upbringing. Those first women and girls who ventured into the program were held in suspicion and talked about. By the time Christian camping had arrived this concept had disappeared; however, it was still a predominately male institution in areas of administration and leadership. A reluctance on the part of the movement to include women in leadership roles has not been to its credit.

When researching the movement of camping in the Mennonite conferences, it would be easy to conclude that women did not play an important role. The stories and actions recorded are too often about what the men and boys did. Thank God for the women and girls who were right in there with the same enthusiasm and dedication as their male counterparts. The following is perhaps typical of how many women and girls may have felt at times: "How can we help? Anyone who has attended an Eastern District Retreat must know by now that there are many girls who have a real interest, and who have the pep to do something about it. Do you know that this interest is just as strong for our Men-O-Lan? We have thus far tried our best to help by just keeping out of the way, and not to hinder the men in the splendid job they are doing. As retreat time is coming closer this interest is getting so strong that we may not be able to hold it from breaking forth. Isn't there some way this enthusiasm could be steered into useful channels? Couldn't we clean the boards, hand up nails, or something, so that we could have a share in the building of Men-O-Lan? Maybe the directors will see their way clear to announce one of these days that we are needed, and our hope can be realized. Signed, one of the girls."[1]

Two women who made significant contributions to Mennonite camping in its formative years were Betty van der Smissen and Edith Herr. Both were associated with colleges on a professional level in the areas of outdoor education and recreation, and brought their professional skills into the Mennonite camping community. It was during the 1950s that their influence was first noticed in a significant way. They brought to the attention of camping people the importance of the outdoor setting to Christian education and its importance as a teaching tool.

In 1957 a subcommittee of the General Conference Mennonite Church Committee on Education met in Chicago to work on curriculum and objectives for Christian camping. The committee consisted of five men and one woman, Betty van der Smissen. Betty's philosophy and contribution to the camping program is contained in the following statement which she helped formulate: "Camping has a special contribution in Christian education because of its direct contact with God's handiwork; its intimate and sustained sharing of life activities in twenty-four-hour-a-day living; its informal, spontaneous, and inspirational approach in programming; and its intimate relationship between Christian leaders and campers."

Edith Herr provided leadership to a dimension of Christian camping that was lacking in the vision of some of the early founders. She was among the first in Mennonite camping to introduce and promote outdoor camping skills as a part of the program. She contended that if we moved our retreats into the outdoors, why not utilize outdoor camping skills as another part of the experience. She made herself available in workshops, counselor training, and as a staff person at summer camps to promote this concept. In 1964, because of multiple sclerosis, she had to limit her participation, but she has continued to be in demand in counselor training and other camping activities even though confined to a wheelchair.

Two other women important to the movement, though in a different way, were Tillie Yoder Nauraine and Alta Hartzler. Both were entrusted with the vision to establish a program for disadvantaged youth, using the outdoor setting as a place and a tool for evangelism and rehabilitation, which each put into practice in different settings. Tillie was concerned with black children from the inner city, and provided a summer camping experience for them. Alta had a concern for boys with problems who needed a chance to make good. She even envisioned a chain of such camps across the church that would be devoted to this emphasis. Mennonite Youth Village, established in Michigan, served many youth over a period of years.

Recognition goes to other women whose names are not mentioned and whose stories of dedication are not told. The movement owes much to their love and caring. They brought to the camps their culinary skills and recipes and Mennonite camping became famous for its good food. The camper was aware that love as well as food was coming from the kitchen. In the cabins, the dining hall, the kitchen, the chapel, the crafts shop, the waterfront, and all across the camp, and at the campfires their voices and skills were making the program complete.

Following the Vision and Unexpected Blessing

The visionary founders of the camping movement in the Mennonite conferences were not aware of the impact the program would have, or of the unexpected happenings that would result from the simple beginnings. They did not dream of establishing a chain of camps across the churches. They saw a specific need in their locality and within their possibility and attempted to meet this need through an outdoor ministry. This gave the movement flexibility, since it could be adapted to many situations in many different ways, and accounted in part for its rapid growth and acceptance. Research does not support the premise that there was a "a founder." No specific individual or group was responsible for its beginning.

These pioneers did not have any doubt about what they were to do, or what their goals were. Their objectives were tailored for the specific needs of the group they were serving. They were successful in working toward their goals and realizing their objectives. The way was being prepared for an expanded ministry, not anticipated in its earliest beginnings.

It soon became apparent that the facilities developed for camping were a gift to the church for the purpose of retreats. Congregations and conferences became aware of the advantages of sponsoring activities in the atmosphere of the outdoors and natural surroundings, away from the everyday world. Retreating had become a necessary function in the lives of many individuals and of the church. Thus many camps developed a two-pronged ministry. They provided facilities and program both for youth camps and for retreats where youth and adults with specialized interests could come for study and fellowship.

Arnold Cressman, a promoter of retreats at Laurelville Mennonite Church Center, wrote in 1979: "Before the end of the decade, let me suggest, retreating will take on the urgency of a parched land begging for rain. What will be needed will be a specific, problem-addressing, frugal, spiritually focused, warmly relational retreat close to home. This suggests a highly decentralized network of small, year-round settings held together loosely by an informal semi-official organization such as the Mennonite Camping Association."[2]

The movement's contribution to evangelism and outreach far exceeded the expectations of its founders. Some camps were founded with this as an objective, but for the most part they were denominationally oriented, and programs were tailored for the youth already within the church. Evangelism was natural in the outdoor setting where living was relaxed and where one was removed from the everyday schedule. Campers began bringing their friends. Christian families brought unchurched neighbors and friends. The ministry of the local congregation was extended to the people of the community who would not respond to its traditional program of outreach and sharing.

Communication between youth and their adult church leaders has often presented a problem. There were no opportunities where young and old could interact in an informal setting such as the Christian camp provided. Those providing leadership and input at retreats and camps became known in a different way. They became real people to the campers. The campers were seen in a different way by adult leaders. This dimension of understanding and fellowship was a source of encouragement and growth to both generations. Friendships and confidence were established that resulted in Christian growth, and a renewed loyalty to the church by its youth.

In the early 1970s the staff at Oaklawn Psychiatric Center at Elkhart, Indiana, were bringing day patients to Camp Friedenswald in Michigan for a twenty-four-hour experience. Here staff and patients enjoyed a dimension of living that could not be duplicated at the Center. The entire group did things together. A staff person could become the blunt end of a practical joke or skit. Patients enjoyed seeing the staff in this situation. They ate together, played together, and dialogued about serious things. The director of the program commented that more was accomplished in this short time than weeks of therapy might provide where all staff-patient relationships were on a professional level.

The Christian camp became an extraordinary leadership training resource for the church. Through the years literally thousands of youth have experienced their first opportunities at Christian service in the church camp. They have been cabin leaders, teachers, and support staff. In many cases this experience has been the motivation for moving into other areas of Christian service to the church. "It is difficult for me to put into words what camping has done to my own life," wrote one person. "I feel spiritually stronger for having experienced those summers in the Rockies. I came to camp that first summer a rather cold Mennonite. The staff and the experience became an inspiration that resulted in spiritual growth." Another wrote, "As I rode home on the bus today I had time to think about and evaluate the week of counseling I had just completed. When I was asked if I wanted to be paid for the week it seemed ironic to me, because it is I who should be paying you. I received so much more than what I gave. Before this week my views on the draft, the church, and life in general were not concrete, and I was aware that I was becoming apathetic. Now I have firm ideas and convictions about life."[3]

Interracial and intercultural camps became common early in the program. Persons with physical and emotional handicaps were included. This provided the church an opportunity to extend its witness beyond what was possible prior to the outdoor ministry of Christian camping. The genius of camping was that its informal setting away from the camper's live-a-day-world contributed to understanding and acceptance of people who were different.

Once on the second day of camp a little boy came into my office with tears running down his cheeks. He was quick to state his problem. "I want you to get all of these 'niggers' out of here right away. If my dad knew they were here he would come and get me out of here yet tonight." When I asked what the problem with them was, his comment was that they were pushing him around. The "niggers" all stayed, the disturbed camper was assured we would work on the problem, and camp went on as usual. I was not surprised when a few days later I observed two boys walking across the camp with their arms around each other, laughing and joking. One was black. One was white. Where else could it have happened?

Cabin grouping can be difficult for camp directors. Campers come from varied backgrounds and ethnic groups. Two Indian boys from the interior of Alaska were having their first experience outside an Indian village. Two boys from Puerto Rico who could speak very little English were visiting in the community. These four registered as campers along with predominantly upper middle-class youth from the Mennonite churches of the area. They were placed in a cabin with four other boys from affluent homes. When the counselor discovered the situation he came to the director asking: "Why me? What am I to do?" These eight boys and their cabin leader became one of the most beautiful and caring groups in the camp. All nine of them experienced learning and appreciation that could not have happened in any other situation.

At Camp Friedenswald in Michigan in the days when racial tension ran high, the Dowagiac, Michigan, schools were processing their sixth graders in an outdoor education program at the camp. There were about 300 sixth graders in the system, and they divided them into three weeks of camping, each staying for five days. Schools in the district were integrated, but some were predominantly white, and others predominantly black. In the out-door program at Friedenswald the groups were thoroughly integrated, with no problems resulting from it.

When Dowagiac children entered the seventh grade they all went to the same large school, and the pattern prior to the outdoor program had been trouble between the races. The first school year following summer camp the faculty noticed a difference in attitudes and acceptance between the races. They concluded that since each year is different, maybe this was going to be one of those better years. But the second year the same situation existed. Blacks and whites had developed a level of trust and acceptance. In these few days at camp they had made some important discoveries. It was possible to relate to people of other races and cultures. What had not happened in one entire school term, could happen in a few days in this informal outdoor setting where living was reduced to simple dimensions, and away from their everyday world. Many a youth has had opportunity to discover the practical meaning of "love your neighbor as yourself" at a Christian camp.

Scattered Mennonite congregations have also benefited from the movement of Christian camping. There are outstanding instances where the development of a facility and program has been responsible for these scattered congregations to discover each other. An example of these would be the churches in Florida that are now known as the Southeast Mennonite Convention. Mennonites began migrating to Florida from many areas of the country. As they established congregations, it was not surprising that they identified with the parent church back home. As a result there was a time when the small and scattered Mennonite churches of Florida represented as many as seven conference districts in the United States. There was no common cause to bring them together, and they remained identified with a conference elsewhere.

The Eastern Mennonite Mission Board was responsible in a large measure for the financial support and leadership personnel for the beginning of the camping movement in Florida. The churches relating to the Lancaster Mennonite Conference were the first to establish a summer camping program as part of their ministry. By 1966 an interest group representing a larger segment of the Florida churches was developing Lakewood Retreat. This project was responsible for helping them discover each other, and over a period of time they developed into one fellowship of congregations working together not only in the development of a camping and retreat center, but in other areas of evangelism and church planting.

In New York state a similar situation existed in the Mennonite congregations, and the development of Beaver Camp and its program became responsible as a factor in uniting these scattered congregations into one fellowship. The establishment of camps and retreats and their program has been a unifying factor where people and congregations have often discovered each other, and have experienced a new dimension of fellowship and strength.

In 1977 Virgil Brenneman, then executive secretary for the Mennonite Camping Association, noted that the camping ministries represent a sizable investment of the funds and personnel resources of the church. He summarized their value as follows:

1. Church camping is education. It is a setting for Christian nurture and evangelism in providing living situations.
2. The church camp is an extraordinary leadership training resource for the church. Youth receive training and experience in counseling, teaching, experiential education, as well as other skills which can be used in other nurture and evangelism settings.
3. The Christian camp is a resource for the church to meet the opportunities and challenge of the "new leisure."
4. The camping program is uniquely suited to model the church's goals with regard to the simple lifestyle, with conflict resolution, the building of the community, and the teaching of the stewardship of creation, and an awareness of a responsibility regarding its natural resources.

A Legacy to Cherish

The pioneers of Mennonite camping were men and women of quality and perseverance. They had a sense of direction, and a call from God. They were satisfied with simple facilities. Only the basics for survival and safety were essential. There was no sophisticated camping gear available. The objectives for camping and the values of the experience did not depend on equipment and buildings.

Now another generation has arrived on the scene. The world in which the founders of Mennonite camping lived and worked has changed drastically. Technology, communication, affluence, the exploration of space and the ocean floor, robots replacing people on assembly lines, these are only some of the changes taking place that will affect trends and needs in camping. The challenge of the outdoor ministry of Christian camping has passed to a new generation, one which has been influenced by the camping ministry, and who on the other hand are products of this changing world. But this outdoor ministry has a genius that does not change. The basic needs of people remain the same. Only the circumstances and influences affecting life experience change.

"The heavens declare the glory of God." This outdoor ministry must be kept out there where the heavens can be seen, where the glory of God is visible, where a relationship to God and creation is possible, where all can become aware of personal relationships to God and the universe. As the trend for facilities with more conveniences is shaping the future of this outdoor ministry, may God grant vision and direction to its leaders and decision makers to preserve the outdoor setting which is so important to the success of the program. God is no closer to those who are worshiping in the atmosphere of a camp or retreat, but they have positioned themselves where they may be more apt to commune with God, to respond to God's voice.

The freedom of the camping movement to experiment with new ideas in program has been one of the factors in its success and growth. It has used this freedom in a reponsible way. It has had the opportunity to reach out and test methods of Christian service and witness. As each succeeding generation assumes leadership this will be a continuing need and challenge.

A leading conference figure in the Mennonite Brethren Church, and who was involved in the camping movement, Rev. Isaac Redekop, summed it up well when he said, "The camp united young and old, and prevented a wider generation gap. It is a monument to the foresight and generosity of an older generation that went to great lengths to produce something primarily for the use of the young; a monument to the young who accepted the challenge and expanded the venture to new heights."[4]

Notes and Acknowledgments

Chapter 1

1. Reported by Frank L. Irwin in 1905, and published first in *Worlds Work Magazine.*
2. Observations made by A. J. Metzler in a taped interview with J. J. Hostetler, 1982.
3. J. C. Wenger, *Glimpses of Mennonite History* (Scottdale: Mennonite Publishing House, 1940), pp. 51-52.
4. Information relating to early beginnings was sketchy, and records were not kept or had been destroyed. Researching numerous files in church archives provided the information recorded here.
5. Harold S. Bender, *Mennonite Encyclopedia* (Scottdale: Mennonite Publishing House, 1955), Vol. 4, p. 657; J. A. Toews, *History of the Mennonite Brethren Church* (Fresno: Board of Christian Literature, 1975), p. 226; S. F. Pannabecker, *Faith in Ferment: A History of the Central District Conference* (Newton: Faith and Life Press, 1967), p. 241.
6. Camp Friedenswald files, Cassopolis, Michigan.

Chapter 2

1. Pannabecker, *Faith in Ferment*, p. 246.
2. Limited information is available relating to the work of the Problems Committee of the Mennonite Church from files in the archives of the Mennonite Church, Goshen, Indiana.
3. Toews, *History of the Mennonite Brethren Church*, p. 227.
4. Information obtained in correspondence with Albert Jantzen, missionary to the Hopis from 1950 to 1970.
5. The Allen Good story is the result of visiting with many persons who were associated with the program, and information from the personal files of Glenn Whitaker. Superintendents who gave leadership after Allen Good include Henry Yoder, Paul Roth, Glenn Whitaker, Marcus Lind, and Claude Hostetler.
6. Pannabecker, *Faith in Ferment*, p. 247.
7. Pannabecker, *Faith in Ferment*, p. 246.
8. Information from files at Archives of the Mennonite Church.
9. Toews, *History of the Mennonite Brethren Church*, p. 228.
10. Toews, *History of the Mennonite Brethren Church*, p. 232.
11. Alan Peters, "A Study of Youth Work in the Mennonite Brethren Church: A Thesis Presented to the Faculty of the Mennonite Brethren Biblical Seminary," 1965, pp. 10-11.
12. Taped interview with Edith Herr, 1982. Archives of the Mennonite Church.

Chapter 3

1. Correspondence from Orie Miller to Paul Mininger, 1934, Mennonite Archives.
2. Wally Kroeker, *Camp Arnes—The First 25 Years*, published by Camp Arnes, 1973. In personal correspondence with the author, permission was granted to share the story as told by his grandfather, A. A. Kroeker.

3. The J. Walter Landis story was compiled from personal interviews with persons who had known him and from Men-O-Lan files.
4. The Glenn Whitaker story is from a personal interview with his wife, Ferne, and son, Warren, and from his personal files made available for research in the Archives of the Mennonite Church.
5. Information from Samuel S. Wenger, *Pioneers Yesterday and Tomorrow*, twenty-fifth anniversary history of Laurelville Church Center.

Chapter 4

1. The Henry Janzen story is from an interview on cassette, 1982, and made available for research in the Archives of the General Conference Mennonite Church.
2. This account is written from the memory and files of the author, and from correspondence with Frank Horst, who was pastor at Culp, Arkansas, at that time. Others who served at Culp include Samuel Janzen, Laurence Horst, George Holderman, Jess Kauffman, and resident workers, Paul Martin, Glen Yoder, VSers Wayne Swartzendruber, Dwight Stoltzfus, Marie Yoder, Marianne Selzer and Harold Bauman.
3. Tillie Yoder Nauraine papers and correspondence are on file at the Archives of the Mennonite Church, Goshen, Indiana. This information was obtained from them as well as from correspondence with persons who had been associated with the program.
4. Additional information on the Larks is available at the Mennonite Archives. This information was taken from the Rehoboth Mennonite Church twentieth anniversary booklet, 1969, and from others who knew the Larks.
5. Alta Schrock provided minutes and reports from her personal files which recorded the vision and earliest actions of the group promoting the program. All information is from this source.
6. George D. Pries, *A Place Called Peniel, Winkler Bible Institute, 1925-1975* (Altona: Friesen and Sons Ltd.), p. 175.

Chapter 5

1. Pannabecker, *Faith in Ferment*, p. 250.
2. Toews, *History of the Mennonite Brethren Church*, p. 283.
3. Report of the Findings Committee of the 1952 Conference on Camping, Elida, Ohio, 1952.
4. From the minutes of the first meeting of interested persons who established Camp Tel-Hai, Pennsylvania.
5. Adapted from Sheila Booker, *Story of Camps with Meaning*, Conference of Mennonites, Manitoba, 1979, p. 23.
6. From brochures and correspondence with Harvey Birkey, 1982.
7. Information gathered from files of the Mennonite Commission for Christian Education at Archives of the Mennonite Church, Goshen, Indiana.
8. Information obtained from Albert Jantzen, veteran missionary to the Hopi Indians.
9. Elsie McDowell, *A Brief History of Fraser Lake Camp 1955-1979*, p. 11.
10. Written from the personal files and memory of the author.

Chapter 6

1. Taken from the files of the Mennonite Commission for Christian Education, Mennonite Archives. Author not identified.
2. McDowell, *A Brief History*, pp. 19-20.
3. Helen Good Brenneman, *Gospel Herald*, Scottdale, Pa., 1958, Vol. LI, No. 38, p. 893.
4. Information from the personal files of the author.
5. Orlo Kaufman, "New Camp Ground Facilities to Serve Churches of Mississippi," *Mennonite Weekly Review*, Oct. 5, 1967, p. 2.
6. *Ibid.*
7. From files and brochures of Bethany Birches Camp, Vermont.
8. From minutes and correspondence of Deerpark files.
9. Information from the personal files of Al Detweiler.
10. Les Engle, MCA Newsletter, April 1979.
11. Taped interview with Jerry Miller, 1982.
12. From the director's journal, Glenbrook Day Camp, Ontario, 1977.

Chapter 7

1. Toews, *History of the Mennonite Brethren Church*, p. 227.
2. *Mennonite Brethren Herald*, Waterloo, Ontario, Feb. 2, 1979, pp. 24-25.
3. Information from the Gardom Lake Camp files.
4. Melvin Delp in *Mennonite Camping Association Newsletter*, Oct. 1975.

Chapter 8

1. From the Camp Men-O-Lan files.
2. Mennonite Camping Newsletter, 1979.
3. From the author's personal files while administrator at Camp Friedenswald in Michigan. This and the following illustrations come from the author's personal experiences.
4. Kroeker, *Camp Arnes*, pp. 26-27.

Acknowledgments

To the many camping people who responded to requests for information.

To the following Archives and their staff for cooperation and valuable assistance:
  Archives of the Mennonite Church, Goshen, Indiana
  Mennonite Library and Archives, North Newton, Kansas
  Center for Mennonite Brethren Studies, Fresno, California
  Mennonite Historical Library, Bluffton, Ohio

To all members of the Mennonite Camping Association Executive Board for their support and valuable suggestions.

To Ivan Kauffman for assistance in editing and guidance in format and design.

To Mary Erickson for artwork.

Appendix A
Mennonite Camp Statistics—1920-1980

Established campsites with facilities and program (1982):

Mennonite	41
General Conference Mennonite	18
Mennonite Brethren	16
Brethren in Christ	10
Evangelical Mennonite Brethren	1
Total	76

Established programs with annual activities in leased facilities (1982):

Mennonite	8
General Conference Mennonite	1
Mennonite Brethren	5
Total	14

Grand total of facilities and established programs: 90

Forty-six facilities and programs using leased and improvised facilities out of the past have been phased into other programs and camps or discontinued after serving their purpose. A total of 136 camps and programs were researched, beginning in the 1920s.

Membership of participating Mennonite bodies (1982):

Mennonite	110,320
General Conference Mennonite	60,267
Mennonite Brethren	39,836
Brethren in Christ	15,096
Evangelical Mennonite Brethren	3,965
Total	229,484

Capacity of camps and retreat centers (1982):

Mennonite	4,800
General Conference Mennonite	2,500
Mennonite Brethren	2,300
Brethren in Christ	3,217
Evangelical Mennonite Brethren	160
Combined capacity	12,977

Acreage owned by camps and retreat centers (1982):

Mennonite	4,299
General Conference Mennonite	2,062
Mennonite Brethren	1,694

MENNONITE CAMPING PROGRAMS BEGUN 1920-1980

This map shows the approximate location of all the 106
permanent camp and retreat programs established since 1920.
Some have since been combined with other programs,
or have been discontinued.

■ Permanent facilities
O Improvised or leased facilities

Brethren in Christ	791
Evangelical Mennonite Brethren	60
Combined acreage	8,836

Annual operating budgets of camps and retreat centers (1982):

Mennonite	$11,500,000
General Conference Mennonite	1,066,000
Mennonite Brethren	2,020,000
Brethren in Christ	632,000
Evangelical Mennonite Brethren	137,000
Combined annual operating budget	$15,355,000

Book value of camps and retreat centers (1982):

Mennonite	$18,000,000
General Conference Mennonite	3,583,000
Mennonite Brethren	8,443,700
Combined book value	$30,026,700

Current value of camps and retreat centers (1982):

Mennonite	$34,000,000
General Conference Mennonite	8,500,000
Mennonite Brethren	10,732,000
Brethren in Christ	5,137,000
Evangelical Mennonite Brethren	700,000
Combined current value	$59,069,000

Ratio of camps, retreat centers, and established programs per member (1982):

Mennonite	1 for each 2,828 members
General Conference Mennonite	1 for each 3,172 members
Mennonite Brethren	1 for each 1,897 members
Brethren in Christ	1 for each 1,510 members
Evangelical Mennonite Brethren	1 for each 3,965 members

Appendix B
The Development of an Inter-Mennonite Camping Association

The Mennonite Camping Assocation was born out of a need that was felt among camping people very early in the movement. Prior to an inter-Mennonite fellowship, each conference of Mennonites provided various kinds of opportunities for their camps and leaders to get together for sharing, and in conferences for developing leadership. The beginning programs did not have personnel who had experienced camping as young persons. This made these times of sharing important in giving program the direction it needed. The General Conference Mennonite Church held conferences for the promotion of the outdoor ministry of camps and retreats and for training leadership as early as the 1940s. Some of the literature that resulted from their studies benefited all Mennonite camping.

The Mennonite Church became active through its Commission for Christian Education in the early 1950s. In the Mennonite Church the camps were being established by independent interest groups, rather than by the conference. They formed their own associations for purchasing, developing facilities, and for program and philosophy. This was not the trend in the General Conference Mennonite Church or the Mennonite Brethren. They usually had their roots within a recognized agency of the church. This independence exercised by the Mennonite Church camps may have been responsible for the Commission for Christian Education not providing a supporting role as quickly as camping people desired.

As each group of Mennonites wrestled with the problem of leadership training and the sharing of techniques, a beautiful thing was happening that was not visible at the time. There were a few who had the vision of an inter-Mennonite fellowship of camps and camping people. They had so much in common. Why not get together to share and affirm each other? What is now the inter-Mennonite fellowship known as the Mennonite Camping Association took shape over a period of several years.

During the decade of the 1950s, camping in Mennonite circles was receiving attention and leadership from people with professional training, as well as others with a keen insight for its potential. As early as 1947 the Church of the Brethren held a national conference on Recreation and Camping to which Mennonite camping leaders such as Helen Mueller, Erwin Goering and Os wald Goering were invited. Bob Tully, associated with camping in the Church of the Brethren, was also being used in Mennonite circles to give leadership in camping and retreats. Outstanding leaders in the outdoor ministry of the Church of the Brethren who provided input were persons experienced in camping such as Al Brightbill, Dan West, and Russel Helstern. This conference was in session for several days, and it is credited with having a tremendous influence on the direction of camping and retreating in the Western District of the General Conference Mennonite Church. Bob Tully, who at that time was on the Bethel College faculty, and a coach, directed the post-war camping programs and was the driving force to acquire Camp Mennoscah at Murdock, Kansas.

A camping committee appointed by the General Conference Mennonite Church was active during the 1950s and prior to the organization of the Mennonite Camping Association in 1960. They sponsored several conferences on camping and retreating and produced some helpful manuscripts. Betty van der Smissen, Oswald Goering, and others have continued their involvement in camping over the years and have related nationally to groups such as the American Camping Association, National Council on Outdoor Education, Christian Camping International, and other professional organizations.

It was from this group that the idea came for the Conference on Recreation and Camping which was held on the Goshen College campus, in November 1956. Later in the 1950s one was held on the Bethel College campus dealing with curriculum. Roman Gingerich and Edith Herr, both on the Goshen College faculty were active in providing leadership and input in Mennonite Church camping. It was persons like this who took graduate work in camping and outdoor education, and who were responsible for training leadership within the camping community.

The following step-by-step outline of the formation of the Mennonite Camping Association was researched by J. J. Hostetler from the files of the Mennonite Commission for Christian Education at the Mennonite Archives in Goshen, Indiana:

1951: The Mennonite Commission for Christian Education appointed a committee to invite interested camp associations and camping people to a conference to evaluate the camping ministry, and to discuss needs and direction. Roy Koch, J. J. Hostetler, and A. J. Metzler, planned and led the conference at the Salem Mennonite Church, Elida, Ohio, January 1952. At this meeting it was the consensus of opinion that the Commission should establish the office of secretary of Church Camps.

May 1952: Mennonite Commission for Christian Education appointed a committee with Roy Koch, chairman, Paul Shank, Frederick Erb, and Edith Herr to plan a second conference of interested camps and camping people. This conference was held at the Prairie Street Mennonite Church, Elkhart, Indiana. Again it was proposed that a secretary of Church Camps be appointed.

April 1953: Mennonite Commission for Christian Education took action to appoint a secretary of Church Camps, and authorized another conference to be planned by Roy Koch, J. J. Hostetler, and A. J. Metzler.

October 1953: Roy Koch was appointed as secretary of Church Camps for a term of two years. Additional conferences

132   Appendices

were authorized, as well as gatherng statistical information and the promotion of Christian education in the camp setting.

October 1955: Jess Kauffman was appointed to serve as secretary of Church Camps for a period of two years. This appointment was renewed in 1957, and in 1959. In January of 1961 Virgil Brenneman was appointed as assistant, and in April of 1961 took office as the secretary of Summer Camps.

February 1956: A conference on camping was held in the Jefferson Street Mennonite Church, Lima, Ohio. There the proposal was made that camp fellowship be organized to bring camping interests and concerns to the attention of camping people.

February 1958: The fourth camping conference was held in the Science Ridge Mennonite Church, Sterling, Illinois. At this conference a philosophy for church camping that had been prepared by Jess Kauffman and Paul Lederach was generally accepted and approved.

April 1958: Action was taken to approve planning for a churchwide fellowship of people in Christian camping. J. J. Hostetler and Jess Kauffman were appointed to develop ideas and plans how Mennonite Commission for Christian Education and such a fellowship would relate.

August 1958: Jess Kauffman and J. J. Hostetler met and developed plans for the proposed fellowship, outlined a tentative constitution, and proposed plans for implementing the same. October 1958, the Commission received the report and took action to authorize the establishment of the camp fellowship and to bring it into being.

February 1960: The fifth conference in the Mennonite church on camping was held at the Zion Mennonite Church at Archbold, Ohio. The fellowship was discussed and the tentative constitution approved. In March of 1960 the Commission approved the proposed constitution for the association of camp fellowship, and took action to participate as a full member. They asked Jess Kauffman, J. J. Hostetler, and Levi Hartzler to convene camp representatives and interested persons at the August 7, 1960, Sunday School Convention for the purpose of bringing this fellowship, which would be the Mennonite Camping Association, into being. A number of interested people met, with Jess Kauffman as chairman, and approved the constitution. Charter members signed the first membership roster, and officers were elected as follows: Roman Gingerich, president; Vernon Schertz, president-elect; John D. Zehr, secretary-treasurer; Roman Stutzman, fourth member; Jess Kauffman, fifth member. The date for the first annual meeting was set for February 1961.

March 1963: The Mennonite Camping Association Executive Committee requested Virgil Brenneman to serve as their executive secretary on a one-fourth basis; with employment beginning June 1, 1963. His assignment was to edit a newsletter, establish training courses and workshops, promote regional and annual meetings, visit camps for counsel, and serve as a clearinghouse for personnel.

The possibilities and advantages of an inter-Mennonite fellowship of camping interests was gaining momentum as the vision of several camping leaders. Dan Graber, director of Camp Friedenswald in Michigan, a General Conference retreat center, was among the first to advocate the inter-Mennonite fellowship. In 1963 the original constitution was revised to include camps other than those originally included in the organization. Dan served as its president for a two-year term after this merger. From this beginning it has grown into a beautiful example of cooperation by the Mennonite bodies working together to provide their people with meaningful spiritual experiences in an outdoor ministry, complementing the program of the local congregations.

It became evident in the early years of the Association that the potential for its services to the camping ministry was far more than it could accomplish. The services of a part-time staff person contributed to the success and the growth of the Association, but were not sufficient to make all the objectives possible. There was also a variety of opinions from camping people as to what the priorities of MCA should be. Those serving over the years as executive secretaries were John Smucker, Edith Herr, and Virgil Brenneman. Their directives came from the executive board of MCA, with whom they worked closely.

A list of objectives established in the 1960s represent the goals and objectives of MCA as they related to the outdoor ministry of Christian camping in the Mennonite camps of North America. They were stated as follows: (1) Provide opportunities for fellowship and sharing of information and ideas, needs and resources, inspiration and know-how, experience, and personnel. (2) Publish and distribute a newsletter. (3) Sponsor conventions, workshops, leadership training programs. (4) Collect and share camp and related source materials and helps. (5) Develop a personnel resource file of experienced camp persons to be resources in workshops and leadership training. (6) Explore and promote good camping procedures which maximize the outdoor setting for Christian education. (7) Develop criteria for evaluation and development of curriculum. (8) Develop and refine camping philosophies which support the Christian educational philosophy of the church. (9) Maintain liaison relationships with the Christian education boards of the church. (10) Interpret and promote Christian camping as integral to the total educational ministries of the church. Where feasible promote camping through cooperative advertising and interpretation. (11) Expand the fellowship and service opportunities through MCA to include leisure time ministries for families camping on their own, vacation and travel experience, congregational retreats and the leisure interests of senior citizens.

The Association was instrumental in bringing camping people together for sharing and affirmation. Directing a camping facility and program could be a lonesome job. It was easy to lose a sense of direction. Participants at these gatherings often returned to their work-a-day world with new vision and enthusiasm, as well as with new ideas and tools for working. Like a campfire, the log that rolled off to a side soon went out, but a lively campfire resulted when the pieces were close together. The program was kept on course as leaders dialogued. They looked again and again at the purpose and philosophy in relation to the Anabaptist theology of brotherhood, peace, and servanthood. They kept alive the theology of creation. They encouraged one another as they discovered they had the same problems and the same concerns.

As many camping facilities were developed for retreats for families and interest groups, camping people recognized that the original concept of "reducing life to simple dimensions in the out-of-doors as the key to Christian camping" was no longer possible at the camps and retreat centers. Each year they became more comfortable with added conveniences and services. Even though most campers seemed to prefer the stay-put experience, camping leaders were promoting away-from camp experiences to add a dimension to Christian camping that could no longer be attained in the traditional campsite. The fellowship and sharing that was experienced through MCA enabled this phase of the outdoor ministry and encouraged its success and growth.

Mennonite Camping Association provided the channel through which the concerns of the outdoor ministry could be communicated to agencies of the church, as well as to the church at large. It also provided the church the opportunity to speak to Christian camping regarding concerns they might have. It was the vehicle representing all the camps and the camping movement in relating to the educational agencies of the church, as they cooperated in the Christian education program, complimenting each other.

In the mid 1970s the executive board was dealing with some concerns regarding the direction and purpose of the Association. The December 1973 Newsletter carried this article: "The MCA agenda involves a number of weighty issues. One is the evaluation of MCA itself. There are two streams of concerns which come together in MCA. One is that of fellowship, sharing ideas and manager types of concerns. The other is that of philosophy of camping, the ability to look critically at our program in light of our goals. The first set of concerns are addressed at regional conferences. . . . In the second area of concern it will be necessary to involve the Christian educators of the church in the outdoor ministry. . . . There seems to be little challenge or guidance given to camp boards by the district education committees."

It was May 1978. The Executive Board of MCA was in session at Waterloo, Ontario. On the agenda was the future of MCA and its structure. The minutes record: "We continually struggle with finances. It is clear that we need a change of structure. Camps do not want MCA to die. Since the major part of the budget goes to staff salary, it is likely this position will need to be altered or dissolved as of November 1978." This was the beginning of some difficult decisions for the board. The dialogue on the structure of MCA got under way in 1977 at the Executive Board meeting. The discussion centered around the questions: "Does the structure of MCA need to change? What are some models we should look at? What is the relationship of MCA to the conference educational boards?" It had become evident that some camps and conference boards were concerned. The Commission on Education of the General Conference Mennonites had withdrawn official support. Camps were asking whether MCA with its present structure could provide the services necessary within the budget they had established.

November 1978. "The MCA Board at a meeting in Elkhart, Indiana, on November 12-13 has undertaken a serious assessment of its present status and services in light of its current record of income and expenses and in light of its future services to Mennonite church camping. The board recommends to the MCA membership the following: (1) That the MCA Board function primarily to plan self-supportung biennial conventions, plus regional workshops on the off-years, with other services being curtailed. (2) That MCA discontinue at present the office of executive secretary. (3) That MCA release the denominational Christian education boards from further financial subsidy of MCA and urge each of them (a) to continue and expand their interest and support of church camping as an integral part of

congregational ministries and (b) to provide for their representation on the MCA Board by a staff person charged with church
camping interests."

This decision was disturbing to many camping people. Why
was it necessary to discontinue the MCA staff and services? MCA
was unable to get financial support from the camps or from the
churches at large. A leading figure in the founding of Mennonite
camping, Betty van der Smissen, then president of the American
Camping Association remarked: "It is regretful that the
denominational Christian education boards do not see fit to
financially support the outdoor ministry of the church to the
extent necessary, and in fact to enhance the ministry. It is especially interesting, perhaps significant, that church camping is
the fastest growing segment in the camping field today, as evidenced by the CCI and ACA . . . yet the Mennonites are seemingly
having to take a major step backward!" Ron Rempel of the
Mennonite Brethren expressed himself thus: "I respect and support the decision of the board to curtail MCA services for the
present. It seems as though the board has done its best in trying
to act responsibly. But a question comes back to trouble me. If we
can pull off inter-Mennonite efforts in publishing, in service and
missions, why has the effort in camping developed such a bad
limp?" John Nissley of Tel Hai Camp comments, "Based on
personal experience, and not on theory, I believe that Christian
camping is one of the most, if not the most influential and
dynamic programs affecting youth in our church."

It was not the end of the road for MCA; it was just a bend in the
road. Camping people rallied to its support. Both regional and
churchwide conventions continued to prosper. The Newsletter
was published in another format. The personnel provided by the
various Christian education boards on the Executive Board of
MCA gave it an added dimension of inspiration and strength.
Persons became available to provide services on a voluntary
basis. Camping people who found fellowship at the various gatherings became a family of brothers and sisters, knowing that they
were involved in one of the great ministries for the nurture and
evangelism of youth.

Appendix C
The Development of a Philosophy in Mennonite Camping

"The organized summer camp is the most important step in
education that America has given the world." This oft-quoted
statement was made in 1916 by President Charles W. Eliot of
Harvard University. This was prior to the time when churches
had become active in the movement. Educators and agencies

were responsible for the growth of organized camping, but churches were soon to follow and benefit from this institution for learning. A few years later the Methodist Board of Education published the following: "The most significant development in Christian education of our generation is the rapid growth of the church camping movement of America. The nature of camping is such that it offers opportunities for learning through outdoor living, healthful recreation, experience in cooperative living and spiritual enrichment not duplicated elsewhere. Even in the experimental stage of church camping, leaders have recognized the ease and rapidity with which changes come in the lives of the campers. The camp affords continuity of experience in a controlled environment. Likewise, in camp, learning through experience is speeded up because of the camper's readiness to learn. This camper readiness is assured."

In the earlier beginnings of camping in our Mennonite camps there was little attempt to verbalize and spell out a rationale. Those early pioneers seemed to have a built-in knowledge of its potential, and the necessary ideas for making it work. There was very little literature available that explained the significance of what they were doing. They were sometimes accused of being overly optimistic about what the outdoor ministry of Christian camping had to offer. Years later when a philosophy was written that came out of years of experience, it did not contain any surprises. Those early leaders in the movement were on target.

It was their common practice to have a set of objectives and goals, either written or unwritten. Those persons promoting the outdoor ministry had many questions to answer. The objections and criticisms directed toward the movement required them to take a second look at what they were doing. Were they being realistic in thinking that Christian camping was important to the nurture and evangelism of youth? This led to the development of a written statement that would speak for the entire movement as well as for the specific camp. Camping people, and others in the church, were also aware that the camping movement was closely related to other educational agencies within the church. Their relationships must be recognized and understood by all concerned. Camping people were probably the first to verbalize that camping had a unique mission in the field of Christian education, and that it must both understand and confine its ministry to that which it could do best, and not attempt to merely duplicate what the church was already doing.

The early attempts at written statements of purpose and philosophy were by camp directors for their specific programs. Typical is one written in the early 1950s: "Experience has proven that parents and pastors do not send children to camp so they can hike, play, have fun, live in the wilderness, and have a good time in general. They send them for those spiritual values and plus contributions that church camping can make in their lives. Unless church camping lives up to its claims, it cannot exist, and should not. . . . Camping is a part of the total program of the church, and is not intended to replace any of its existing teaching agencies, but to compliment them. Its nature is such that it offers teaching and learning opportunities that cannot be created in any other situation. In this atmosphere the camper can develop positive attitudes toward problems, self, the church and its leaders, and God. In the warm and spiritual atmosphere of a church camp youth find answers that put them in tune with their creator."[1] The statement continues to support the rationale and suggest ways and reasons why this happens to youth at camp. It is evident that the statement was the result of questions and objections that had been raised.

In 1956 a Recreation Study Conference was sponsored on the campus of Goshen College, Goshen, Indiana, and a paper was read on "The Place and Relation of Church Camping to the Total Recreation Program." The paper endeavors to establish the premise that church camping has its own unique place to fill in the program of education and evangelism within the church. "Church camping does have a rightful place in the work of the church, and it must assume that responsibility. It came into being to meet a need, and because it does provide a better way and a better place for certain activities important to nurture and evangelism. The natural and informal setting of the camp lends itself to teaching situations that are favorable for learning. In this informal, relaxing atmosphere the camper will often face up to basic problems of life and find answers. Positive attitudes are formed that result in spiritual growth. The ultimate objective of camping is to produce in each camper a deeper appreciation of God, church, and others; and to contribute to a deeper appreciation of the real values in life. This, in short, is the unique contribution of Christian camping to the total ministry of the church. It must produce spiritual growth. The recreational program of the camp must contribute toward this ultimate goal."[2] This conference was sponsored at a time when both recreation and camping was being questioned by some within the church. Opponents of the camping movement were wary that recreation could become its major goal.

One of the first attempts at formulating a philosophy was sponsored by the Mennonite Commission for Christian Education, and approved by a representative gathering of camp people at a conference on church camping at Sterling, Illinois, March 1958. Following is the text of the philosophy:

Camping as a spiritual ministry of the church is designed to be an integral part of our total teaching and evangelistic effort. It seeks to serve and make its contribution in those areas for which it is best adapted.

The environment of the local church and its program is best suited to most phases of nurture and evangelism. However, other aspects of nurture and evangelism can be more effectively realized in the outdoor atmosphere and living together experience of a good church camp. Those things that can best be taught in the local church program should be taught there; and the camp's program should include primarily those features, and employ such teaching techniques, for which it is best suited. The "indoor" and "outdoor" ministry of the church is not competitive; but rather they strengthen and complement each other.

Camps, like other educational agencies, deal in four categories of experience; namely: skills, habits, attitudes, and teaching of facts. Of these four, church camping is intended to make its greater contribution in the development of Christian attitudes. Its natural environment and Christian atmosphere provide an excellent context for making this contribution. The other three experiences are not ignored, but implemented only as being incidental to meeting the ultimate objective of church camping; namely to help the camper recognize and correct harmful attitudes in the various phases of life through a confrontation with Christ and his will, and to learn to rely upon divine resources to strengthen desirable attitudes and convictions.

It has been proven by experience that this is camping's outstanding and unique contribution to the ministry of the church. It is important that program content and teaching technique be tailored to meet this objective. Campers who come and go from our camps must return with wholesome attitudes toward God, toward their church, toward their home, and toward their own personal conflicts or problems. Mental blocks that retard spiritual progress are often removed through a camping experience in a Christian atmosphere.

The outdoor setting of a camp provides for simple living close to God and to nature. This setting is in contrast to the tensions and competition of everyday life. Rubbing elbows with fellow campers and Christian leaders twenty-four hours of each day makes possible rich experiences of living together. These experiences are unique to camping, and are responsible for its effective ministry. Church camping provides many opportunities for initiating and encourging change in attitudes, behavior, and spiritual understanding.

This statement was lengthy and attempted to cover many things. It spoke of the relation of this outdoor ministry to the church. It pointed up the relationships of camps and local congregations. It spoke to the contribution it made to the camper. It outlined the unique characteristics of the movement. It stressed the fact that the indoor and outdoor programs of the church were not in competition with one another, but that their purpose was to complement each other. It was important at that time to state all of these things. They were in answer to questions that were being asked. Both camping people and church leaders in Christian education were asking questions and seeking answers.

In 1960 the Mennonite Camping Association was organized and grew to include the major Mennonite bodies in Canada and the United States. This larger representation of camps and camping people represented many years of experience in varying situations. They had opportunitiy to test program techniques and observe results. Statements of philosophy were often on the agenda in gatherings of camp leaders. In 1970 at one such gathering called a Conference on Camping Philosophy, a group representing the inter-Mennonite community of camps and retreat centers worked for two days discussing philosophy and rationale for the outdoor ministry of Christian camps. Dr. Robert Tully, camping leader in the Church of the Brethren, was invited to guide the process. At one point during the conference the participants were divided into nine small groups, and using the guidelines established were to come up with a brief statement of philsophy. They read as follows:

1. Through Christian camping the Mennonite church seeks to help all persons to know God as revealed supremely in Jesus Christ, the Scriptures, and in all creation. This is experienced uniquely in the camp setting through the five senses, through interpersonal relationships, and through understanding the stewardship of all of God's resources, both natural and personal.

2. Organized camping can be an effective teaching and learning situation if the genius of camping is recognized and utilized. The unique characteristics contributing to this genius are the natural setting, small group of peers in continuous living, informality and openness of leadership, and the simplicity of camp life. Getting away from the pressures of home and school provide learning situations where life can be tested.

3. Christian camping is a living laboratory located in a natu-

ral setting where campers and staff work together to develop a Christ-centered type of life which has meaningful understandings and relationships to nature, to themselves, and to others.

4. Christian camping is an effort to provide a living experience in a unique atmosphere, the out-of-doors, where people can relate to each other through loving and caring; learning to know and care about the lives of others in a way that communicates the love of God.

5. We believe that Christian camping is an experience in an outdoor setting, in which people recognize Jesus as Lord of all creation and live together in an openness to all that his Spirit reveals through other persons and through the world about them.

6. Camping is an interchange of an interpersonal relation with God's world and God's people in the out-of-doors. Within this setting the campers can discover themselves in their relation to God, to nature, technology, and to others in group living experiences.

7. Camp is a specific period of time away from regular routine activities, to explore and discover under the lordship of Christ oneself, others, the environment, and God. This discovery leads to the end that campers adopt values, priorities, and a style of life that will not exploit others or the environment.

8. Camping focuses on learning through living relationships in the context of experiencing nature as interpreted and understood in the light of God's Word in Christ. Thus programming and counseling take seriously the natural environment, with a view for cultivating appreciation for it, developing skills in using it, caring for it with a sense of stewardship, responding in the worship of God who created it; and second, interpersonal relationships, including crisis situations, as an agenda for growth in self-understanding and Christian community.

9. Through the Mennonite camping program, we seek to assist the individual to discover, accept, and move toward a God-given potential for all of life in Christ. The outdoor setting provides the context in which Christian values are explored and developed in real life situations through interpersonal and group experiences.

These statements are presented here with a minimum of editing, and represent the thinking at that time. They refer to the basics such as the outdoor environment, the stewardship of creation, evangelism, the small group learning and living together, and growth in the total person as a preparation for meeting life and its problems.

A condensed statement that has recognition in many of the

camps came out of this conference and the sharing of nearly a hundred participants at Goshen, Indiana, in 1970:

Christian camping focuses on learning through living relationships in the context of experiencing nature as interpreted and understood in the light of God's Word. Thus programming and counseling take seriously: First, the opportunity of confronting campers with Jesus Christ and commitment to his way of life. Second, interpersonal relationships in real life situations as an agenda for growth in self-understanding, acceptance of others, wholesome attitudes toward one's self, the church and the world. Third, the natural environment, with the view to cultivating appreciation for it, developing skills in using it, caring for it with a sense of stewardship, and responding in worship to the God who created it.

Ten years later, in 1980, a group of camping leaders representing fifteen denominations met at Camp Hanover in Virginia for twelve days to ask and answer questions such as: "Why church camping?" They developed a statement as follows:

Church camping is one viable and effective means for furthering the ministry of the church. Provided with a living experience in a "place apart" over an extended time, persons are enabled to explore God's story, to experience the vitality of Christian community, and to grow in the faith. Church camping helps bring about the reconciliation through Christ of one's self, to God, one's neighbor, and the environment. Through its programs, persons are encouraged to discover who they are and why they are responsible for their communities and the world in which God has placed them. With the leadership of responsible Christians, this community is challenged to experience lifestyles which may serve as prophetic models for all of God's people.

Probably the philosophy for camping has been written a hundred times by that many people. It will continue to be written and rewritten to meet changing times. In 1880, George W. Hinkley, who is given credit for the first church camp, had a philosophy too. It is recorded like this: "Believing that the informality of camp living would break down barriers, he took seven of his church boys on a camping trip, sponsored by his church. He realized his aim to know his boys better and influence them toward God."

---

[1]Reported in *American Camping Magazine*, 1980.

[2]Reported in Sargent's *Handbook of Summer Camps*, 1935. Published by the author. Copies available in Library of Congress, Washington, D.C.

About the Author

About his experience in the camping movement, Jess Kauffman says, "My experience in this movement began in the 1930s out in the Colorado Rockies. I was in my early twenties and had been ordained to serve as a minister in a country church at Cheraw, Colorado. The congregations of that area had sponsored some youth gatherings, usually known as Young People's Institutes. It was only a hundred miles to the mountains and the scenic beauty of Manitou Springs. Why not take our institute to the outdoors? That is what we did, using the local church as the headquarters. That was the beginning which was to set the direction for my life, and my career in the church."

Since that summer in 1935, Jess has spent a part of each year in Christian camping and retreats. He served as camp administrator at Rocky Mountain Camp in Colorado, at Camp Friedenswald in Michigan, and at Lakewood Retreat in Florida. He assisted in many short-term experiences in various places. He served as secretary of church camps under the Mennonite Commission for Christian Education for a number of years and worked with many camp boards across the church as they looked for sites and worked on camp development and philosophy.

During the 1950s Jess was led into a program of rehabilitation with delinquents, using the setting and philosophy of Christian camping. This continued on either a part-time or full-time basis for fifteen years. During this time he was involved in the beginning of two year-round rehabilitation centers for boys, Frontier Boys Camp, later known as Frontier Boys Village, and Brockhurst Boys Ranch.

Jess, now retired, lives in Brookville, Florida, with his wife, Viola.